# PROTECTING
# AND
# REBUILDING
# YOUR
# RETIREMENT

# PROTECTING

# AND

# REBUILDING

# YOUR

# RETIREMENT

---

Everything You Need to Do
to Secure Your Financial Future

Les Abromovitz

AMACOM

American Management Association

New York • Atlanta • Brussels • Chicago • Mexico City • San Francisco
Shanghai • Tokyo • Toronto • Washington, D.C.

*This publication is designed to provide accurate and authoritative information in regard to the subject matter covered. It is sold with the understanding that the publisher is not engaged in rendering legal, accounting, or other professional service. If legal advice or other expert assistance is required, the services of a competent professional person should be sought.*

*Library of Congress Cataloging-in-Publication Data*

*Abromovitz, Les.*

    *Protecting and rebuilding your retirement : everything you need to do to secure your financial future / Les Abromovitz.*

       *p.   cm.*

   *ISBN 0-8144-7185-4*

    *1. Retirement—Planning.   2. Finance, Personal—United States.   I. Title.*

   *HG179.A253 2003*
   *332.024'01—dc21*

                                             *2003001415*

*Printing number*

*10  9  8  7  6  5  4  3  2  1*

Retirement planning is much more enjoyable when you're sharing your plans and dreams with that special person in your life. My wife, Hedy, and I have been planning and dreaming about retirement since we were married nearly 29 years ago.

Health problems can undermine your retirement plans. My Dad's retirement ended too soon for all of us last year. My Mom is bravely moving forward through retirement without him. My sister, Phyllis, and my mother-in-law overcame serious health problems, and are once again enjoying retirement with their husbands. My sister, Pam, can't wait to retire, and all of us, including every reader, will hopefully enjoy a long, healthy, and satisfying retirement.

# CONTENTS

WHEN YOU'RE TRAVELING LATE AT NIGHT IN AN UNFAMILIAR AREA, YOU head down the wrong road. Instead of getting closer to your destination, you move farther away by the minute. To make matters worse, you may be frightened, anxious, or sleepy, and your gas tank may be nearing empty. If you're really having a bad night, it might start to snow or rain heavily.

Retirement planning, especially now, may remind you how it feels to be lost and frightened in an unfamiliar area. You thought you were heading in the right direction but now you're not sure. Even though you're growing older, retirement appears to be getting farther away.

During the past few years, you may have opened up your 401(k) retirement savings plan statement and found you lost more in one quarter than you made in salary. Or maybe you didn't open your investment statements, because you didn't want to see the bad news. Younger workers look at their dwindling 401(k) retirement savings plans and believe they'll never be able to retire. Discouraged by what they see, these young employees drop out of their employer's savings plans and give up on saving for retirement.

There are people who are a lot worse off. They worked for companies like Enron and WorldCom. Their companies went down the tubes, thanks to mismanagement and shady accounting practices. Worse yet, many of these employees faced the double whammy of having too much money tied up in company stock that became worthless.

When your employer goes belly-up, you might face additional problems. If your severance pay is paid out in installments, a corporate bankruptcy might put a stop to those checks. You may find that you are out of work and out of money and your retirement savings are decimated. If you're already retired, you might lose any money you have in your employer's stock, as well as any health insurance coverage paid for by your former employer.

Even if your employer or former employer is financially sound, your retirement may still be in jeopardy. A bear market can undermine your investments. Low interest rates can cut your income enormously. Inflation and taxes can eat away at your savings. You're also in danger of fraud or mismanagement of your nest egg.

*Time* magazine posed the question, "Will You Ever Be Able to Retire?" in a cover story on July 29, 2002. The magazine cited eroding pensions, longer life spans, and a major meltdown of stocks as reasons why many people will be working until they drop and why retirees are jumping back into the labor pool.

Sticking your head in the sand is not the answer. Sure, you can stop reading the financial pages of the newspaper and listening to business reports on the radio or television. You can avoid opening your 401(k), IRA, and other financial statements. You can head for the mall to spend money and forget about your financial problems. Or you can take an expensive vacation with the hope that you'll forget about the fact that your retirement plans are eroding.

The problem, however, is that you can run but not hide from the impact of financial turmoil on your retirement. Ignoring your financial statements is like getting a report card you know is bad and not looking at it. You know the report card is bad, but you don't want to face it. Similarly, ignoring the bad news in your financial statements will undermine your plans for retirement, and you'll never be financially secure.

Hopefully, you're ready to deal proactively with the problem and take steps to protect your retirement. Whether you're young or old, nearing retirement or already retired, you can reach the goals you've been working toward over the years. You don't need a global positioning system or high-tech solutions, just a road map that's easy to follow.

In the chapters that follow, you'll learn how to invest your money for the best and worst of times, even if your knowledge of personal finance could fit in your glove compartment. You'll discover ways to guard your pension and retirement savings plan, as well as your IRAs. You'll learn how to avoid running out of money and how to keep scam artists from funding their retirement with your nest egg. You'll also find out how to protect your retirement from the risk of needing long-term care, as well as huge medical bills.

If you're already retired, you have other options aside from "unretiring," and we'll look at them. You may decide to work in retirement, but it should be a choice, not because you're forced to earn an income. Retirement should be a time when you can pursue new dreams and perhaps a new career, but the decision shouldn't be driven by money.

If you're still working, you shouldn't be forced to postpone your retirement. There are ways to grow your retirement nest egg and move forward as planned. You can protect and rebuild your retirement, so you can retire and "unretire" when you're ready.

This book is not for you if you see yourself as someone who knows how and when to buy and sell stocks. It's also not for readers who think they can predict when the stock market will go up or down. This book is for anyone who took a hands-off approach to retirement planning in the past and got burned. You learned the hard way that buy-and-hold doesn't mean investing and then forgetting about it.

It's become clear that a passive approach to retirement planning won't work. You need to become actively involved in protecting your retirement. Taking control of your retirement planning doesn't mean you have to be a sophisticated investor and know all of the investment terminology. Each chapter will cover the basics, and you'll do fine if you just keep your eyes on the road ahead.

There is more to this book than just protecting your retirement. It's also about protecting your peace of mind. Peace of mind is far more important than whatever you're making on your investments. Without peace of mind, your retirement isn't going to be very enjoyable.

Even if you got lost on the road to retirement over the past few years, or you're already retired and moving backwards, you can still find your way before the sun rises again. All you need is a road map that anyone can follow. So, before you go any farther in the wrong direction, stop and look around. There will be many more financial storms in our lifetime, and if you don't learn to act decisively, the next one might totally wash out your road to retirement.

## ACKNOWLEDGMENTS

MANY PEOPLE HAVE BEEN EXTREMELY HELPFUL IN THE PREPARATION OF this manuscript. In particular, I would like to thank Ray O'Connell, Mike Sivilli, and all of the folks at AMACOM. I'm also grateful to Kathie-Jo Arnoff, who made many valuable editorial suggestions.

# PROTECTING
# AND
# REBUILDING
# YOUR
# RETIREMENT

# CHAPTER 1

# It isn't too late to
# protect your retirement

IN A COLUMN CALLED "ECON 101: SUPPLY, DEMAND, AND PRAYER," humor writer Dave Barry answered this question: "I have noticed that the longer I stay alive, the less money I have saved for retirement. Why is this?"

Barry responded, "You probably have a 401(k) plan, which is a type of plan where your balance gets smaller each month and eventually disappears altogether, like pizza in a men's dormitory."

Barry's observation may not strike you as funny if your 401(k), IRAs, and other retirement plans were devastated by the bear market. If you're retired, you've probably slashed your budget, and dinner at a pizza joint now seems like a luxury. If you're still employed, you face the possibility of working for years longer than originally planned.

If you love your job, postponing retirement isn't the worst thing that can happen. Walter Cronkite has been quoted as saying he regrets giving up his career. Since retiring over twenty years ago, the veteran CBS anchorman has felt a desire to return to work every day. Cronkite said in an interview that he could have worked much longer and still had time to spend with his family.

After you've been retired for twenty years or more, it's easy to look back and say you could have stayed in the workforce for much longer. Unfortunately, you can't predict if your retirement will last twenty years or twenty days. Furthermore, you may not love your work as much as Cronkite did. When you come home from work, perhaps you're too exhausted to do anything but watch the evening news. At the end of every day, you may be more than ready for retirement.

When the economy is doing poorly, it's hard to unwind in front of the evening news. You may have lost more money that day in the stock market than you earned last month. Although your inclination is to tune out the real world, protecting and rebuilding your retirement means facing up to the financial and psychological problems that can undermine your future.

## FACING UP TO RETIREMENT REALITIES

The decline of the stock market in the early part of the twenty-first century has caused many people to chuck their retirement lifestyle. *The New York Times* reported that Jim and Jan Pringle were sitting pretty in terms of retirement. They sold their advertising agency for more than $2 million and invested the money. The couple was looking forward to retirement at a time when the Dow was well above 10,000. By July 2002, however, they lost 75 percent of their investment and decided to unretire. Instead of taking some time to travel and to contemplate their next move, the Pringles went back into the advertising business.

Many retirees have similar problems. Their portfolio is a fraction of what it once was. Instead of working to keep busy and stay active, they are returning to the workforce out of necessity, not choice. Unlike the

Pringles, these retirees may not be able to return to their previous line of work.

If you're already retired, you may be having problems, even if you're not in the stock market. Interest rates are low, and living on a fixed income is harder than ever. You may be depriving yourself and your family to pay for prescription medicines, as well as other expenses that can't be avoided.

Budgeting for retirement isn't an exact science. Until you decide what your retirement lifestyle will be and where you'll be living, you can't nail down what your outgo will be. Some financial planners estimate that you'll be spending 60 to 80 percent of your preretirement income. There's another rule of thumb that predicts your living expenses in retirement will be 70 to 80 percent of your preretirement spending.

Those estimates will come as a shock to the people who responded to a survey conducted by Strong Capital Management. Fifty-nine percent of the people surveyed in 2001 did not expect to cut back on their current lifestyle in retirement.

A study for the TIAA-CREF Institute found that roughly 55 percent of the people surveyed expected spending to drop in retirement. About 36 percent thought it would stay the same and 8 percent predicted spending would go up. According to the study, about 30 percent of retired households are spending less. Twenty-two percent are spending more, and about half reported that their spending was unchanged.

The reality is that many retirees find their expenses are the same or greater than what they once were. They're spending more money on travel, golf, eating out, and movies because they have more free time. One personal finance magazine reported that a couple spent $40,000 on travel in one year, an expenditure that put a serious dent in their retirement savings. Even if you give up travel, however, you may still be in danger of exhausting your savings.

The years prior to retirement are extremely important for most people. It's when you usually earn the most and have your major expenditures behind you. Your pension, if any, is often based on the highest three years of earnings in your last five. It's also a time when you're usually contributing more to 401(k) retirement savings plans. Unfortunately, however, if the economy sours during that time frame, you risk losing your job, and your investment portfolio might be ruined.

Any age is a bad time to get sick, but the risk increases with each birthday. If you're working, you've already noticed that health insurance costs are skyrocketing, and your employer is probably picking up less of the bill. If you're out of work, you may be buying insurance from your former employer, and it's not cheap. COBRA, otherwise known as the Consolidated Omnibus Budget Reconciliation Act of 1985, usually permits you to buy coverage from your former employer for eighteen months or more, depending upon your situation.

With COBRA, you're paying the full group rate, and you don't get the employer's contribution. In addition, there is usually an administrative charge of 2 percent. According to the Kaiser Family Foundation, the average employer-sponsored health insurance plan cost $7,954 in 2002 for family coverage.

Retirees have their own health insurance issues. When companies do poorly, they're inclined to cut back on health insurance benefits for retirees. The cost for retirees is likely to go up, even though they're on a fixed income and may be making very little on their investments. Worse yet, a number of companies are now eliminating health insurance coverage for retirees. For example, on February 6, 2003, Bethlehem Steel asked the bankruptcy court for permission to eliminate health insurance coverage for substantially all of its retired workers and their dependents.

Women in particular will have problems protecting their retirement. They live longer than men and earn less on average. Frequently, they rely on Social Security for most of their retirement income. Women often lose years of earnings while they're raising a family and acting as caregivers for elderly parents.

## WORRYING ABOUT RETIREMENT

Author and *Wall Street Journal* columnist Jonathan Clements wrote that it is a misconception that bear markets destroy wealth. If you add fresh savings, according to Clements, bear markets give the opportunity to create wealth. Although Clements is correct, it certainly looks like your wealth is gone when you open your 401(k) statement or hear on the news that the investors have lost trillions of dollars since the beginning of the bear market.

Obviously, a bear market can destroy your wealth if you liquidate your stock holdings when your shares are at their lowest value in years. Even seasoned investors can be tempted to sell with each report that stocks are headed steadily lower. When seemingly solid companies like Enron, WorldCom, and Adelphia declare bankruptcy, it's easy to fear that your holdings may follow the same path. And if you're not sleeping at nights, it's tempting to get out of the stock market while you still have your shirt, home, and other things you value.

Another psychological issue is when you feel you're throwing good money after bad with your investments. If you invest on a regular basis in a stock or mutual fund, you may not miss the money if it's deducted automatically from your checking or savings account. Nevertheless, when you get your statement and your account is worth less than what you've put in, it's tough to convince yourself to keep investing. Your inclination is to stop investing each month and put the money somewhere safe.

Psychologists who study money issues will tell you that people are very different when it comes to financial matters. That's one big reason why investment temperaments differ from person to person. It's another reason why protecting your retirement isn't a one-size-fits-all approach.

Let's look at a very simple example. If someone tells you that you'll need to spend less because your investments aren't earning as much, how do you react? Some people will curb their spending, because they know that small savings add up. Others will take the position that it's pointless to cut spending, because that strategy isn't going to put them back where they once were financially, so why bother? And some people may agree that cutting spending makes sense, but they need to indulge themselves so they can forget about their financial dilemma.

Another distinct difference among people is that some have a live-for-today mentality, while others need to know that they have enough money to live on until they hit age 120. The live-for-today group is willing to withdraw as much money as they think they need from their nest egg, even though it might be exhausted long before they die. The second group consists of worriers. They live in fear that there won't be enough money available when they need it. Typically, the people in the second group are reluctant to make a dent in their nest egg and won't spend more than their earnings, if that.

No matter which group you happen to be in, there are ways to achieve your goals and maintain your financial peace of mind. You must, however, keep an open mind and be willing to change.

## RIDERS ON THE STORM

When the bear market hit, many investors were riders on the storm for the first time. Young investors in particular were not ready for rough water. Like novice sailors, they didn't realize how violent the sea could become.

It's easy to chastise people by saying, "You shouldn't be an investor if you're not willing to ride out the storm." With equity investments, you need to expect volatility. Nevertheless, many investors were not expecting as much volatility as they got during the recent bear market.

The problem too is that you can't ride out certain storms. If you've invested too much in one or two stocks and those companies go under, you can't ride it out. You'll sink to the bottom.

Assuming your boat is still afloat, your goal is to sail forward. If you're young, there's time to correct your course. If retirement is no longer a distant dot on the horizon, you have less time to shift directions. And if you're already retired, you're looking for a safe harbor. Whichever category you fall in, you need the wind at your back as you go forward toward a more peaceful financial existence.

The stock answer to people who ask how to protect their retirement is to stay invested. Don't panic, you'll be told. Focus on the big picture and try not to get upset over short-term fluctuations in the market. Stock answers, however, won't necessarily help you sleep at night or correct the damage done to your portfolio.

## THRESHOLD QUESTIONS

As you put in place a plan to protect your retirement, there are some basic questions you need to answer.

## When do I want to retire?

If the answer is never, you must have picked up this book by mistake. But if you do plan to retire someday, you need to look at your ideal retirement date and the age when you actually can retire.

Most people think about retiring when they feel they have enough to live on for the rest of their lives. These people look at the amount of income they can expect from Social Security, a pension, and their investments. The problem with investments is that they might be worth a lot more tomorrow or a lot less. Because of the recent bear market, most people are finding their investments are worth a lot less than they used to be.

## Where do I want to live in retirement?

Too many people make retirement plans without any idea where they want to live in retirement. You need to narrow down the possibilities.

Your current home may seem perfect right now, but maintaining it may be a great deal more difficult down the road. Those high property taxes that you paid to support the great school system might not be as easy to swallow now that your children have received their diplomas.

Trading down from a big home to a small one is a common strategy, but don't bank on those profits yet. Your present home may not sell for what you're expecting, and the price of your new one might creep up. The dream house you're looking at may have more bedrooms than you need, all the latest features, a pool, and a much higher price tag than the one you're in now.

At a minimum, figure out what state you're going to live in after you retire. Once you've done that, you'll know what to expect to pay in state, local, and property taxes.

## What will it cost to live in retirement?

No rule of thumb can determine how much your retirement lifestyle will cost. You won't be able to predict the cost of your lifestyle in retirement until you decide where you want to live. If you plan to stay in the same house and live roughly the same lifestyle, you should have a clear picture of what retirement will cost. If you plan to live elsewhere, there are many variables in the equation.

The cost of your lifestyle will also depend on the activities you intend to pursue. If you'll be watching the Food Network all day, it will be a lot less expensive than taking cooking classes in Paris. Some retirees have dreams but they don't know where to start when it comes to planning for them. They need to budget how much it will cost to pursue those dreams.

## How will I spend my time in retirement?

A large number of retirees leave the workforce without any plan for how to spend the next twenty to twenty-five years, let alone the next twenty-four hours. They're not used to being around their spouse or life partner 24/7.

Money issues can exacerbate any problems that may arise from being together too much. For some retired couples, spending time together means spending money. As couples adjust to life without a paycheck and being on a tighter budget, they may begin to argue over money. While one may be content to sit down with a good book from the library, the other pursues more expensive activities. If they're spending too much time together and money is tight, the quality of their relationship is likely to suffer.

Without a plan, you're likely to be bored and depressed. Being busy isn't enough. The activities must give meaning to your existence. Many retirees struggle with feelings of self-worth. Their identities were tied to their former professions.

## INOPPORTUNE TIMES TO RETIRE

In the middle of a bear market, one couple moaned that they picked an inopportune time to retire. Their current house wasn't selling and their investments were doing poorly. They had already committed to building a new home in Florida. The wife complained that if they had known how bad the economic climate would be, they would have kept working.

Unfortunately, hindsight is 20/20, but you have to play with the cards you're dealt. And sometimes, you've dealt those cards to yourself.

If your timing is bad, you can put your retirement in jeopardy. For example, you may be a buyer during a seller's market. You are likely to overpay for a home in a sizzling hot housing market. At the same time, the home you're selling might be in a less desirable area, and house sales are flat. The end result is that because of bad timing, you might find yourself trading up to a more expensive home in retirement, rather than trading down to a cheaper dwelling.

Bad timing can't always be avoided. You're in the middle of repairing your house and your car breaks down. Or maybe you're short of cash and you suddenly need a root canal and crown that isn't covered by insurance. Ideally, you have a rainy day fund to cover those unexpected expenditures that seem to happen all at once, but the timing is frustrating nonetheless.

## TAKE CONTROL OVER THE TIMING
## OF YOUR DECISIONS

To protect your retirement, you need to take control over the timing of important decisions. Selling your house, buying a new home, and quitting your job need not occur simultaneously at the moment you retire. If your current house doesn't sell, you're stuck with two homes and no job. And if your investments are tied up or are doing poorly, you will find yourself in a situation that's out of your control.

The search for the perfect retirement house takes months or even years. Assuming you're moving to a totally new area, you should leave enough time to thoroughly investigate the housing market and make a good deal. Don't put yourself in a position where you're buying the first house you see out of desperation or laziness. You may want to wait for the closing on your current home before putting money down on a new one, even if it means living in an apartment for a while. If you do buy that new home before you're sure your current house is sold, hold off on retiring, so you won't drain your nest egg.

Set an absolute limit on how much you'll pay for the new home. It's easy, especially when you're building a home, to allow the cost to creep up as you opt for a no-edge pool, nicer cabinets, and lots of other extras. If you're not paying cash for the home, place a cap on how much you're willing to pay each month. Don't buy any house until you're sure what the property taxes, maintenance fees, insurance, and mortgage-related costs will be.

Don't buy too big a home in paradise just because your kids will come for a visit once or twice a year. If where you're living is a great vacation spot, a huge home may attract scores of unwelcome guests. Unless you're a glutton for punishment and love to entertain, you don't want to make guests too comfortable or they'll stay the winter.

Although you may be an optimist, protecting your retirement requires you to realistically plan for worst-case scenarios. Instead of planning for everything to fall into place at exactly the right time, develop a strategy that doesn't require all events to occur on the exact day, month, or even year. If your health is starting to slip, start looking at housing options that will work better for you later in life.

## A NEWLY RETIRED COUPLE'S TIPS FOR MAKING THE TRANSITION TO RETIREMENT

Avoid putting too much on your plate at one time. Avoid retiring, moving, selling your old house, and building a new one at the same time.

Don't stop working abruptly.

Maintain work contacts and stay involved in professional organizations and trade groups. Keep all doors open.

Start reinventing yourself before you retire, so you'll avoid losing your identity and sense of self-worth.

Have a plan for fighting inertia and lethargy. Avoid a sedentary lifestyle. Engage in activities that will help you to feel productive. Keep those intellectual juices flowing with continuing education courses and hobbies that keep your mind active.

Give your partner enough space, so you're not together 24/7.

## DRESS REHEARSALS

Retirement involves a number of physical, psychological, economic, and professional adjustments. Knowing what to expect is half the battle. One couple hated the thought of retiring, because it meant they were entering the last stage of life. Retirement meant facing their mortality.

The reality is that you face your mortality every day, whether you're retired or not. Whether you're 40, 60, 80, or older, your days are numbered. You have to decide for yourself if you want to spend them in retirement or at work.

The Financial Planning Association (www.fpanet.org) suggests having a dress rehearsal for retirement. After envisioning what retirement life will be like, the organization recommends that you try out your retirement lifestyle. You should take a long vacation and live each day as if you've already retired.

Your dress rehearsal should include your spouse or life partner. Retirement is a 24/7 proposition, so spend each day together. The two of you should rehearse living on your retirement budget for several months.

The Financial Planning Association also advises that you rehearse for retirement by semiretiring. Retiring isn't as easy as it seems. Working part-time helps you ease into retirement. It helps to cut back hours or start a new job that's less demanding. You can use the extra time to rehearse what full-time retirement will be like.

## PROTECTION TIPS

To protect and rebuild your retirement, you need a blueprint to follow. Studies show that the people who are happiest in retirement planned thoroughly. You should love talking about retirement and planning for the day it comes. You're not wishing away your life, just building your future. When you plan for retirement, you're envisioning your dreams and creating a plan to bring them to life.

For most people, the ideal retirement means being healthy, both psychologically and physically, and having the ability to live life to its fullest. You can look back on your life with satisfaction and forge ahead toward new goals.

To reach that plateau, it helps to have more than you need to live on for the rest of your life. Retirement is much more satisfying when you feel secure financially. It's certainly much better than worrying whether you have enough to live on in the near term and down the road when you're reading the large print version of this book and others.

To protect and rebuild your retirement, you need to be meticulous in planning for the future. Don't make any impulsive decisions regarding retiring, quitting your job, or moving. Wherever possible, test the water before making irreversible decisions.

# CHAPTER 2

# Protecting and rebuilding your retirement nest egg

Some people have very modest plans for retirement. There's a T-shirt that captures their retirement lifestyle. The T-shirt says, "I'm retired. I'm up, I'm dressed. What else do you want?"

Whether you have simple or grandiose plans for your retirement, you'll need money to live on. Even if your retirement wardrobe consists entirely of T-shirts, you'll still need a nest egg to supplement your Social Security benefits. Unfortunately, Americans aren't doing a very good job of saving for their retirement. The average savings rate, which wasn't good to begin with, has been declining since 1992. According to the Commerce Department, the savings rate of Americans hit a new low of 1.6 percent in 2001.

In the past, people could rationalize their poor savings habits by pointing to how much they were making in the market. Their net worth was increasing, even though they weren't saving much. The bull market made

13

them overlook how little they were saving. And it also made them overlook the amount of risk they were taking with their money.

To protect your retirement, you need to look inwardly. You must perform an honest appraisal of your attitudes toward saving and investing. Saving is the act of putting aside money for a particular purpose. Investing is the process of making your savings grow. Building a nest egg requires that you understand the psychological and economic factors that have an impact on your ability to save and invest.

There are many Internet sites that can help you calculate what you need to save to fund a comfortable retirement. Financial planners also have software to estimate how big your nest egg will grow to be. All of these projections rely on you to keep saving and investing through good times and bad.

To get a ballpark estimate of what you need for retirement, the American Savings Education Council (ASEC) has come up with one of the easiest worksheets to use. It can be found at www.asec.org/ballpark. The worksheet assumes you'll live to age 87 and will need 70 percent of your current income. The ASEC's Ballpark Estimate also assumes your return on investments will be 3 percent after inflation is taken into account.

## FROM RISK TOLERANCE TO RISK INTOLERANCE

Investors learned a great deal about their risk tolerance in the early 2000s. Risk tolerance is the ability to cope with the inevitable ups and downs that go hand in hand with almost every investment. If you look at the business page in the newspaper each morning and get depressed about your losses on paper, you have a very low tolerance for risk. If you realize that paper losses are just paper losses, your tolerance for risk is a little higher.

Risk tolerance seems to go out the window when the market suffers a steep decline. Harold Evensky, a financial planner in Coral Gables, Florida, has been quoted in the *South Florida Sun-Sentinel* as saying that people have an infinite amount of risk tolerance as the market goes up. Their risk tolerance lasts about ten seconds when the market goes down.

Peter Lynch, in a CNBC interview with Maria Bartiromo on August 19, 2002, discussed how different investors are. Some investors view 20 percent of their money in stock as aggressive investing. For others, aggressive investing is having 80 percent of their money in stock.

Someone who is risk-averse is better off sacrificing a higher rate of return for peace of mind. An individual with a high tolerance for risk accepts swings in the market as a necessary element to achieve a high rate of return.

If you've been burned by the stock market or some other investment, you may become more risk-averse. If you have income coming in from a variety of sources, you're likely to be more risk-tolerant. There's no need to panic when your investments decline significantly in value if you have income from a number of other sources.

As you get older, there's a tendency to shun risk. It's harder to deal with volatility, because you may need to tap your investments soon. You know your days in the workforce are numbered, and there's less time to recoup your losses. Furthermore, as your wealth builds, you have more to lose, and you may find it harder to deal with volatile investments.

## HOW LONG WILL YOUR NEST EGG LAST?

Assuming we're in good health and our minds are alert, most of us want to live as long as possible. The downside, however, is that you may outlive your money. When you spend too much of your assets too quickly, you risk reaching old age with very little income.

If you're like most people, you enjoy watching your net worth grow each year. Retirement, however, is a time when you start enjoying the fruits of your labor. There's a good possibility that your nest egg will get smaller, not larger.

Some retirees are never able to comfortably shift from a saving mode to a spending mode. Even if their only income is Social Security, they want to live on it and squirrel away a few bucks. Whether it's the fact that they lived through the Depression or came from a poor background, these people always worry about having enough.

There are many others who should be worried, but aren't. They are withdrawing too much money to live on and risk exhausting their nest eggs. As they age, it's less likely they'll be able to go back to work to rebuild their fortune. These retirees face the possibility of living out their sunset years with financial problems.

Even mathematicians who are ready to retire may find it difficult to decide with absolute certainty how much they can safely withdraw. The Monte Carlo methodology is a mathematical approach that examines 500 potential market scenarios and determines whether your withdrawal rate will exhaust your nest egg. Using software based on this methodology, you can calculate how much can be withdrawn without running out of money.

With the Monte Carlo simulation, you see a range of potential outcomes. For example, there might be a 99 percent probability that you can withdraw $1,000 per month and never exhaust your nest egg. There might only be a 60 percent probability that you can withdraw $2,000 per month without exhausting your nest egg.

The Schwab Center for Investment Research offers a guideline that for every $1,000 you want to withdraw monthly, you need to have assets of $230,000. Therefore, if you want to withdraw $3,000 per month, you need to own assets of $690,000. Schwab's figures presume that you'll take out this amount for forty years and it will be adjusted for inflation. Furthermore, it presumes your funds are invested in a moderately aggressive portfolio.

Assuming you prefer a more conservative portfolio, Schwab recommends that you have $340,000 for each $1,000 per month withdrawal. Therefore, that same $3,000 per month withdrawal requires you to have assets of $1,020,000.

The problem with all withdrawal projections is that they're based on assumptions. They presume that future returns from certain investments will be in line with historical returns. These projections also make assumptions about inflation, tax rates, and how long the person will live.

Many experts don't believe the stock market will achieve the same high levels of return in the coming years. In a retirement program on public television, aired on Labor Day in 2002 and produced by *The*

*Nightly Business Report* and WPBT2 in Miami, Florida, two well-regarded experts predicted that stock market investments won't reach their historical average of 11 percent down the road. Harold Evensky and Roger Ibbotson viewed 9 percent as a more realistic rate of return.

To avoid exhausting your nest egg, it pays to err on the low side in the early years of your retirement. You should take out no more than 4 percent of the initial value of your retirement portfolio. That percentage can be adjusted upward or downward each year, depending upon how your investments are performing.

Suppose you start out with $400,000 in your retirement savings. Your first-year withdrawal should only be about $16,000, even if your rate of return is more than 4 percent. Ideally, your nest egg will get larger during the early years of retirement as you reinvest earnings in excess of what you're withdrawing. This is necessary to fend off inflation. As you reach the later stages of your retirement, you can withdraw more from your portfolio and spend more of the principal.

Some readers and financial planners will argue this point. They contend that younger retirees need more income, because they lead a much more active lifestyle. They will need less money ten or twenty years from now.

In theory, your spending needs do diminish as you age. In the earlier stages of retirement, you're on the go much more. You're traveling and spending more on recreational activities.

The counter argument is that younger retirees are usually in better shape to work and earn income. Therefore, they need to draw less money from their nest egg. You might also argue that you'll need more money in later years for long-term care and other health-related expenses.

No rule of thumb works for every retiree. Some retirees still love to travel at age 85, while others didn't like to travel at age 65. You need to look at your specific financial situation. Furthermore, in view of the recent bear market, it seems clear that no one should base his or her rate of withdrawal on too high a rate of return.

Instead of using a rule of thumb like 4 percent, it's best to discuss your situation with a financial adviser or to use a computer program that calculates how long your money will last. Many financial websites provide interactive calculators, so you can calculate how much you can spend without blowing all of your money.

**WEBSITES THAT LET YOU CALCULATE HOW LONG YOUR NEST EGG WILL LAST**

Financial Engines, www.financialengines.com

Quicken, www.quicken.com/retirement

Whether you're using a financial planner or doing it yourself, make sure the calculations are based on a realistic rate of return on your investment. Most people need to plan on their retirement lasting twenty-five years or more. If your life expectancy is short, you can take out a larger percentage.

You also need to look at your dependable sources of income. If most of your needs are met by a pension, an annuity, and Social Security, there is far less danger of depleting your assets.

## UNCRACKING YOUR NEST EGG

Even if you've already started withdrawing from your nest egg, you still have time to recover. You must, however, take decisive action to correct your situation.

If your calculations show that you're withdrawing too much, here are a few of your options:

- Increase your investment income.
- Return to the workforce on a full- or part-time basis.
- Withdraw less.
- Cut your living expenses.

## Increasing your investment income

Increasing your investment income is easier said than done. In theory, you can invest more aggressively, but that's no guarantee, and you might actually put yourself in an even worse financial situation. Nevertheless, there are investments that can make your nest egg work harder for you without putting it at risk.

You can also shift the risk to someone else. For example, annuities can ensure that you don't outlive your income. You may select a payout option that will continue for your lifetime, no matter how long you live. You can also arrange for a lifetime income for a spouse or some other beneficiary.

## Returning to work and withdrawing less

Going back to work or staying in the workforce protects your nest egg for a number of reasons. First of all, you're not tapping your investments, especially at the worst possible time. Suppose you own 1,000 shares of a blue-chip stock that's fallen from sixty dollars per share to thirty dollars per share. Let's say you need an extra $12,000 to live on this year and must sell shares of that stock to get the money. You need to sell 400 shares of that stock to come up with the money you need. In better times, you would only need to sell 200 shares.

The fact that you're working helps you avoid liquidating any shares. Or it might postpone the time when you need to liquidate those shares. Hopefully, they'll be back at sixty dollars when the time comes that you need to sell.

By going back to work or staying in the workforce, there's another advantage. You might be able to increase your savings, which will allow you to safely withdraw more at a later date.

There's a final reason why going back to work or staying in the workforce protects your nest egg, and it's a disheartening one. It cuts the number of years your savings need to last, because you'll be that much closer to the time when you won't need any money anymore.

Obviously, there's an inherent contradiction in the above statement. It's almost like saying that the only way to protect your retirement is to not retire. Once again, it's one of many options for protecting your retirement, not the only one. Work should be a choice, rather than the only means of protecting your retirement.

## Cutting your living expenses

Another option is to make spending decisions that don't put your money at risk. Each dollar you don't spend means less money coming out of your nest egg. You'll be far better off if you cut your spending before retiring, rather than after. You have more money to save and you become accustomed to living on less.

## PROTECTING YOUR RETIREMENT FROM OUT OF CONTROL SPENDING

Comedian Jackie Mason is mystified by the success of Starbucks. He pictures the founder coming up with this great new idea for a coffee shop. In Mason's comedy bit, the founder says, "Instead of sixty cents for coffee, I'll charge $2.50, $3.50, $4.50, and $5.50. Not only that, I'll have no tables, no chairs, no water, no busboy." You clean up after yourself and pay for refills. Amazingly, Mason observed, someone said, "That's the greatest idea for a business I ever heard."

If you can't imagine retirement or any morning without your Starbucks coffee, don't worry. You're not going to hear the standard advice about how much you'd save by giving up gourmet coffee. Nevertheless, according to *Physician's Money Digest*, saving and investing the five dollars per day you spend on coffee, cigarettes, or alcohol will build a nest egg of $403,166 in thirty years, assuming an 11 percent average annual return.

To a large extent, you control how your money is spent, but there are many things in life we can't control. Certain health problems can't be prevented, no matter how healthy a lifestyle we lead. We might be involved in an accident that's not our fault, or we might be the victim of violence.

The fact that we never know what fate awaits us is justification for some people to spend money. Life's too short, they argue, to deprive ourselves. Almost any expenditure is justified because we might not be around tomorrow.

The problem with this live-for-today justification is that it generates guilt and worry after the deed is done. These people lose the peace of mind that comes with knowing they have enough to live on down the road. If protecting your retirement is a priority, you're someone who wants the peace of mind that comes with having enough money to live on for the rest of your days.

Protecting your retirement is difficult if your spending habits are out of control. How you spend your money is something you can control to a large extent. No, you can't necessarily control your healthcare expenses, but most expenditures are your decision. You decide how much to pay for a house. You decide what kind of car you want to drive. You decide what your lifestyle will be.

While most people are willing to spend less in retirement, they don't want a drastic change in their lifestyle. Protecting your retirement doesn't have to mean giving up all the amenities you're used to, but it may mean scaling back. If every element of your lifestyle is too important to give up or scale back on, your choice is to keep working or risk exhausting your nest egg.

Often, the best time to scale back is while you're working, not after you retire. For example, a busy professional takes up golf. He has the most expensive set of clubs you can buy and a membership at an exclusive country club. All that's missing is the time to golf. When you add up the dues and other expenses of the country club, as well as the bond, each round of golf costs him a fortune.

According to the Club Managers Association, country club dues average $4,000 per year. There's an average one-time initiation fee of $27,500. If you live in a climate where the golf season lasts about six months and you only get out to the links a dozen times per year, you might do better playing golf at a good public course or golfing with friends who do have a club membership. A club membership might be a better investment after you retire, especially if you're in a warmer climate and have time to golf several times per week.

To protect your retirement, you also need to curb your children's spending habits. Sociologists have used the term "affluenza" to describe the greed bug that strikes many kids. Children become used to an affluent lifestyle, and their parents don't want to deny them, even if it means their retirement will suffer down the road. In wealthy suburbs, it's not uncommon to see teenagers driving a Lexus, BMW, or Jaguar.

In the early evening in any of a hundred beach communities, there are people walking the beach at sunset. The ocean breeze invigorates them and gives them a sense of inner peace. Often, groups watching the sunset applaud when it sets in the west. In each of those same communities, there are ten times as many people at the mall, buying something they feel they can't live without. You must decide if a few of those shopping sprees can be replaced by activities that don't cost a dime, whether it's sunset at the beach or a walk in the woods on a snowy morning.

Only you can determine your spending priorities. Once you realize the impact those priorities have on your retirement, you might come to enjoy a trip to Costco more than indulging yourself at Neiman Marcus or Saks Fifth Avenue. You need to decide if certain indulgences are worth staying in the workforce longer to have or if they're worth the price of losing peace of mind.

## PROTECTION TIPS

Even though you need a blueprint to secure your future, your plans should be flexible. You need to have a Plan A and a Plan B, as well as fallback plans. You must be willing to revise these plans as economic conditions change throughout your lifetime.

A blueprint won't do you much good unless you're realistic about how much you'll have in retirement and how much you can spend. To protect your nest egg through twenty-five to forty years of retirement or even longer, you need to decide upon a realistic rate of withdrawal. You'll withdraw too much if you base your calculations on making a 10 percent to 12 percent return on your investment. You can't keep presuming a particular rate of return if your investments aren't keeping pace. To play it safe, assume you'll live longer and spend more than you've anticipated. And assume you'll make less on your money.

When your portfolio goes down in value, not up, your withdrawal rate should adjust accordingly. You'll also need to adjust your portfolio in response to changes in the economy and the tax laws. You shouldn't plan on taking out more than 4 percent to 5 percent of your nest egg each year. If you're overextended, you won't be able to cut back on your withdrawals.

At any age, retirement planning begins with a blueprint. If you're serious about protecting and rebuilding your retirement, you have to start now.

# CHAPTER 3

# Protecting your retirement
# from stock market reversals

A *FORTUNE* MAGAZINE ARTICLE ON AUGUST 12, 2002, CARRIED THIS HEAD-
line: "Retirement Plan Stuck in Neutral?" At the time of the article, being
stuck in neutral would have been welcome news for many investors. Their
retirement plan seemed to be stuck in reverse, not neutral.

It's easy to be a raging bull when a bull market is in full swing.
Unfortunately, it's also easy to go into a rage when a bear market engulfs
you. A bull market is a period when investors are feeling giddy about
stocks and are very optimistic. During a bear market, investors are extremely pessimistic and stock prices decline.

Many investors were spoiled rotten in the 1990s. They made nearly
20 percent per year on their investments. Unfortunately, many investment
experts have explained that we're now in a payback period. For the fore-
seeable future, there will be lower returns that will offset the huge gains

made in the 1990s. Seven percent to 8 percent returns are more realistic than the meteoric returns seen during the last decade of the twentieth century.

Chances are, you wouldn't have picked up this book if you were lucky enough to be making a 7 percent to 8 percent return on your investment. More than likely, your investment return has been much lower, your portfolio has declined significantly, and your assets are worth far less than they were when the market was at its peak.

The best way to protect your portfolio from stock market reversals is to keep your emotions in check as you invest. You must have a clear vision of your investment goals and objectives. You also need to understand the appropriateness of your investments for reaching those goals and objectives.

## BACK TO BASICS

A survey conducted by the Investment Company Institute & Securities Industry Association and released on September 27, 2002, found that 52.7 million households and 84.3 million investors own stock or stock mutual funds. Hopefully, these investors possess a basic understanding of how the stock market works.

Let's do some generalizing about the stock market. First of all, the stock market is cyclical. Sometimes stocks are moving steadily upward and other times you want to attack your broker with a sickle.

A bull market follows every bear market, and a bear market follows every bull market. Unfortunately, a bull market won't necessarily follow immediately after every bear market. The market may wander aimlessly in the interim. The good news is that the average bull market lasts about five years, and bear markets stick around on average for about two years. Some bear markets, like the most recent one, stick around much longer.

Since you never know when a bull market will start or end, it's extremely difficult to time your entry and exit from the stock market. Market timing is tough for the experts, let alone most investors. With market timing, you try to jump in and out of the market to maximize your profits.

You put money in when you think the market is ready to explode. You take money out when you think the market is heading downward. The problem is that you really don't know when the market has hit the top or bottom, and it's almost impossible to reliably time when the market is ready to rebound or get worse.

## Common stock

You aren't ready to be a bull or a bear until you understand some very elementary stock market terminology. Common stock is the most basic equity investment. Each share of common stock represents equity in a company. Common stock shareholders participate in the ownership of a company through dividends and appreciation in the value of their stock. They also share in the risk that the price of the stock will go down.

## Preferred stock

Preferred stock is viewed as an income investment, much like a bond. You're buying it for income, more so than growth. With preferred stock, you receive fixed dividends, but no right to vote. In the event a company is liquidated, preferred stockholders are given preference over owners of common stock. And in the wake of Enron, WorldCom, Adelphia, and others, being further up in line helps in the event of liquidation. Nevertheless, bond holders usually have a stronger claim on assets than preferred stock holders.

Preferred stocks, or "preferreds," as they're sometimes called, pay a fixed amount at regular intervals. Normally, the amount is paid every three months but it might be monthly. The dividend is a percentage of the par value, which is the face value of the security. The market sets the price of preferred stock, not the par value.

Most preferred stock is rated as investment grade, which means it's likely that investors will be paid on time. There are independent rating services like Moody's (www.Moodys.com) that evaluate the financial stability of companies issuing preferred stock. These rating services also evaluate the companies that issue bonds.

Like bonds, some preferred securities have a maturity date. Others are perpetual, which means the stock will pay income on an ongoing basis. Nevertheless, the company will be able to call or redeem the stock before maturity. Usually, the company can redeem the stock after five years and pay the investor the face value of each share.

A number of financial experts suggest buying preferred shares that trade for slightly less than the par value. This makes it less likely that the company will call the preferred stock, since it will need to pay the face value of each share, which is higher than the market value.

Preferred shares may be traded easily through a broker. Shares are usually more stable than shares of common stock. The price of each share fluctuates in the same manner as bonds. If interest rates go up, the price goes down. If interest rates go down, the price of each share tends to go up. The price will also fluctuate if investors become worried about the financial stability of the company issuing the preferred shares.

## Tracking stocks

Tracking stocks are tied to a single business within a company. You don't get the same ownership rights as regular stocks. Tracking stocks allow you to invest in a potentially high-growth segment of the company without worrying about the other businesses.

## Mutual funds

According to the survey that was conducted by the Investment Company Institute & Securities Industry Association, more equity investors own stock mutual funds than individual stocks. Eighty-nine percent of U.S. equity investors owned stock mutual funds in January 2002 compared to 49 percent who directly owned individual stocks. Most equity owners cite retirement as their primary financial goal.

Most novice investors are more comfortable owning shares of mutual funds. A mutual fund invests money received from many investors who have mutual goals. The mutual fund is professionally managed by experts who invest in the manner outlined in a company's prospectus. The prospectus is a legal document that describes the mutual fund's objectives, as well as fees, strategy, and other important facts about the investment.

Mutual funds invest in more than just stocks. Mutual funds invest in U.S. Treasury securities, junk bonds, real estate, precious metals, and almost any other investment that comes to mind. Because mutual funds usually have low minimum investments, you can add diversity to your portfolio for a relatively small amount of money.

## YOUR INVESTMENT OBJECTIVES

Obviously, by buying or borrowing this book, you've indicated that your goal is to protect and rebuild your retirement. Unfortunately, your objectives need to be more specific. In a nutshell, there are three investment objectives: growth, income, and safety.

It's hard to generalize about what type of person has a particular investment objective. Younger people are usually still working and don't need to invest for income. They normally have long-term investment objectives. Investing for growth is frequently the best way to achieve those long-term objectives.

The typical retiree needs income, more so than growth. Nevertheless, there is a place in a retiree's portfolio for individual stocks and mutual funds, which are considered to be growth investments. Investing for growth works best, however, when you have a long time horizon and don't need the money for years to come.

When income is a priority, you're normally looking at investments such as bonds, certificates of deposit, and treasury securities. Bonds are loans or debt issued by corporations or governmental entities to raise money. The issuer of a bond agrees to pay bondholders a specified amount of interest and to repay the principal at maturity.

If your investment objective is safety, you often must sacrifice growth and income. Riskier bonds pay more interest. The safest bonds will normally pay less interest. Similarly, the stocks that have the greatest potential to grow in value are far from safe. These stocks have a high level of volatility, which means they can have wide swings in value from very high to very low.

A mutual fund prospectus tells you whether the fund's objective is growth, income, or safety. There are also mutual funds that combine investment objectives. As an example, balanced funds invest in a mixture of bonds, common stock, and sometimes preferred stock. The goal is to blend stocks that will grow in value with securities that pay income from dividends. Usually, at least a quarter of the money is invested in bonds. Balanced funds are less risky than stock-only funds.

## ACTIVE VERSUS PASSIVE INVESTING

During the bear market that began in 2000, it became apparent that even the experts can't always pick great stocks, especially when the pickings are slim. Few investors are able to analyze stocks and prefer a passive investment strategy. Passive investors tend to believe that no one is really able to pick which individual stocks will succeed and rely instead on buying a well-diversified portfolio.

Active investing involves buying selected stocks and stock mutual funds. Active investors switch investments as the economic climate changes. The problem, however, is finding the right investment to buy and knowing when to sell it. In addition, frequent trades often drive up expenses. Passive investors tend to buy and hold investments, which isn't necessarily a good idea.

The strategy of many passive investors is to buy index funds that have low expenses and are well-diversified. An index fund uses the pooled pot of money to match the performance of a broad market index. The fund invests in a shopping basket full of stocks that make up that broad market index.

One well-known index is the Standard & Poor's 500, or the S&P 500, which is a collection of 500 large company stocks. The S&P 500 is viewed as the standard for measuring overall market performance, because it includes many of the top companies in leading industries. In 2002, every one of the ten broad sectors in the S&P 500 dropped. Even the consumer staples sector fell, which was surprising, since it is viewed as a safe haven during tough economic times. In addition to the S&P 500, you can find an index fund tied to many other investments, such as small company stocks, bonds, and foreign companies.

A no-load index fund will not charge a sales commission and will have very low expenses. A no-load mutual fund makes money by charging an annual fee that is deducted from the fund's earnings or added to its losses. The expense ratio, which is the ratio of expenses to assets, shows you how those fees compare to the assets of the fund. A fund's expenses are extremely important, because they reduce your return dollar for dollar. When a fund's expense ratio is low, you get to keep more of the return on your investment.

Index funds usually have very low expense ratios. For example, the Vanguard Growth Index has a 0.22 percent expense ratio. This fund tracks the S&P 500/Barra Growth Index. A Vanguard advertisement shows the difference between investing in a fund that has a 1.3 percent expense ratio and one that has a 0.3 percent expense ratio. According to Vanguard, when you invest $25,000 over twenty years and have a compounded rate of return of 8 percent, you'll wind up with $19,751 more in the fund with a lower expense ratio.

People who advocate active investing shun the passive nature of index funds, even though expenses are lower. They argue that you can't achieve anything more than mediocre returns, because you're tying your fortune to a broad mixture of investments. Nevertheless, there are studies showing that index funds in the long run produce higher returns than many professionally managed mutual funds.

Index funds tend to have fewer tax implications, because there is less turnover of the portfolio. Funds with a low turnover of shares are generally more tax-efficient. In contrast, an actively managed fund usually has a high turnover of shares.

When interviewed by Maria Bartiromo on CNBC, Peter Lynch, the legendary investment expert, explained that investing in index funds isn't a no-brainer. You still need to choose from a variety of index funds. Investing in an index of large company stocks isn't enough, because those businesses won't necessarily be growing as fast as they once did. You'll probably want to add a small company index fund as well and some international stocks.

## HOW TO PICK STOCKS: DON'T EVEN TRY

You picked the wrong book if you want advice on how to select which stocks to buy. We learned from the most recent bear market that even the experts can't pick winners if the market is going badly. If you're someone who believes she can make money trading stocks, you're on your own in protecting and rebuilding your retirement.

When the next bull market comes, many people will forget this advice. They'll believe again that they're capable of finding the next Wal-Mart or Krispy Kreme. Therefore, just as parents tell their kids to avoid premarital sex but urge them to use protection if they do, here are some quick tips to avoid disaster.

First, only invest money in individual stocks that you can afford to lose. You can dabble in stocks if you've protected the bulk of your retirement. Allocate only a small percentage of your wealth toward investing in individual stocks.

Whenever you do invest, know the company whose shares you're buying. It's not enough to know what product or service the company provides. You must also decide if there's a demand for the product or service.

Make sure you understand the numbers. Find out how much the company is worth and understand how much it owes. If you want to read a company's financial reports, go to the Securities and Exchange Commission's (SEC) website (www.sec.gov) and click on EDGAR, which stands for Electronic Data Gathering, Analysis, and Retrieval. Nevertheless, unless you have specialized training, it's difficult to interpret financial data.

Balance the good news with the bad about a company. You may have good reasons for buying a stock, but look at the potential negatives. A company may be working on a promising new cancer drug, but the FDA may not approve it.

Billionaire investor Warren Buffett offered simple advice for deciding whether to buy stock in a company: Before you invest in a stock, understand what a company does. The company must have a favorable outlook. The company must have competent and honest management. The stock must be available at an attractive price.

Peter Lynch believes that picking stocks to buy doesn't require you to be a math expert. He believes you should be able to become an expert on a few companies, especially if they're in an industry you're familiar with, by researching them and following news reports about them. Even experts like Lynch have winners and losers. If you put $10,000 in Kmart years ago, your investment wouldn't be worth anything. But if you also put $10,000 in Wal-Mart, your portfolio would be worth a lot more than the $20,000 you invested originally.

The stock analysts for various financial services firms are experts on certain stocks and industries. It's easy to find their opinion on specific companies and industry sectors. Unfortunately, however, we've learned that stock analysts aren't always objective in analyzing companies. Their opinions are often influenced by relationships their firms have with certain companies. Arthur Levitt, former chairman of the Securities and Exchange Commission, has advised that you never buy a stock just because an analyst recommended it.

StarMine won't tell you if an analyst has a conflict of interest, but it will keep you informed as to which analysts make the most accurate recommendations and which ones make better earnings predictions. StarMine provides independent, objective ratings of Wall Street analysts. You can reach StarMine at 415-777-1147 or online at www.starmine.com.

Financial services giant Charles Schwab now offers Schwab Equity Ratings. It helps investors evaluate over 3,000 stocks with straightforward A, B, C, D, or F ratings. The ratings are based on measures from four broad-based categories: fundamentals, valuation, momentum, and risk. Many other companies offer advice to help you evaluate individual stocks.

## WEBSITES THAT HELP YOU EVALUATE INDIVIDUAL STOCKS

There are several websites that will help you evaluate individual stocks.

ValuePro (www.valuepro.net)

StockWorm (www.stockworm.com)

ValuEngine (www.valuengine.com)

RiskGrades (www.riskgrades.com)

## ASSET ALLOCATION: PROTECTING YOUR EGGS

Before the stock market hit the skids in the early part of this century, asset allocation consisted of putting your money in more than one tech stock. But even if you put your money in a variety of stocks, you were probably burned and burned badly. Asset allocation is a strategy you can use to diversify your portfolio and reduce its volatility. With this strategy, you determine the appropriate mix of stocks, bonds, and cash in your portfolio.

The asset allocation theory should protect your retirement, but let's review the basics. Assets are the things you own that have economic value such as a car or a house. Assets also include your investments such as a bank account or mutual funds. When people refer to asset allocation, they're usually referring to the assets in their investment portfolio, not the asset they drive to work in or the one that provides a roof over their head. There are three broad asset classes: stocks, bonds, and cash.

These asset classes will perform independently of one another during different economic cycles, and that's what makes asset allocation work. Because stock, bond, and cash equivalents have different risks and react differently to market conditions, it's likely that some of your investments will perform well and will compensate for the ones that are performing poorly. Even in bad times, some of your investments will thrive. You're looking for the right balance for your personal situation and investment temperament.

With the asset allocation strategy, you divide your money among different types of assets like stocks, bonds, and cash investments such as money market funds. The way you divide up your investments will depend upon how much risk you can tolerate. If you can't cope with any risk at all, you probably want to stick with a mixture of safe investments such as certificates of deposit (CDs), savings accounts, and bonds backed by the U.S. government. The stock asset class is normally more volatile than the others.

Asset allocation is how you split up the investments in your portfolio. If you're just getting started, you probably have very little money invested, so asset allocation isn't an issue. As your money grows, however, it's important that you diversify your assets, so you're not depending on one or two investments to build your fortune.

Before the market went haywire, financial planners were rethinking the old rules-of-thumb about asset allocation. The conventional wisdom was that you subtract your age from one hundred to determine the amount that should be invested in stocks. For example, a 25-year-old should consider having 75 percent of his assets in the stock market, since one hundred minus twenty-five equals seventy-five. On the other hand, a 60-year-old might want to limit his or her stock holdings to 40 percent, the figure you get after subtracting sixty from one hundred.

When the market was going gangbusters in an upward direction, some financial planners were using 120 as the basis for their rule of thumb. If you followed their advice, 80-year-olds should have 40 percent of their money in stock, since 120 minus eighty is forty.

To protect your retirement, you may want to give both rules a thumbs down. A rule-of-thumb won't necessarily calculate the right mix of investments for your unique situation.

## WHY ASSET ALLOCATION GUIDELINES DON'T WORK FOR EVERYONE

Two 55-year-olds may have different life expectancies. Based on family history, one can expect to live thirty years or more and the other might not be around ten years from now.

All of us have a different tolerance for risk. Some of us cry ourselves to sleep over losing a few dollars in the stock market. Others recognize that fluctuations in the market are to be expected.

Your asset allocation strategy should take other factors into consideration, such as whether both spouses or life partners are employed and how long each intends to work.

Your personal situation may require more liquidity. If you expect to need the money sooner for a major expense such as buying a second home, you should keep more money in liquid investments.

A rule of thumb doesn't distinguish between risky and conservative stocks. Two 50-year-olds may have 50 percent of their money in stock, but one may be taking far more risks.

You can invest more in the stock market if you have dependable sources of income to meet most of your needs, such as Social Security benefits, rental properties, and/or a pension. If you only get some of your income from those sources, you'll need more money from your other investments.

Asset allocation gets more complicated when you break down broad asset classes like stocks into specific asset classes. As an example, you might divide your stock portfolio among large, medium, and small companies. You also will want some money in international stocks. Your bond portfolio should mix conservative securities like government bonds with corporate bonds that are a little riskier.

Even when you invest in a mutual fund that owns a number of stocks, it isn't quite the same as asset allocation. You're still not spreading the risk enough, because your mutual fund might only be investing in certain kinds of stocks and they might not be doing too well at various times. For example, your mutual fund might only invest in large company stocks, and that's not enough diversification.

Many financial experts believe that having the right mixture of assets is more important than picking a great stock or mutual fund. If those assets do well, chances are you'll do well, even if you don't happen to buy a stock that goes through the roof or the top-performing mutual fund.

Even as you invest in different kinds of assets, you still need to be liquid. Having an emergency fund of three to six months' living expenses is not enough. You don't want to be forced to sell assets like stock to pay unexpected bills. It might take five to seven years for the stock market to regain all of its losses from a bear market.

It's not just unexpected bills that affect your asset allocation strategy. If you know you'll need to sell assets at some point to pay for a wedding, the down payment on a house, or some other purchase, you may want to keep a smaller percentage of your money in stocks. Otherwise, you might be forced to sell some of your stocks when the market is down.

There are mutual funds that try to diversify your assets for you. An all-weather fund is designed to perform well in all phases of a market cycle. The fund manager creates a diverse portfolio with low and medium-risk investments. An all-weather fund invests a fixed percentage in stocks, bonds, real estate, and cash investments. Some all-weather funds invest more aggressively in stocks and bonds, depending on the outlook for these investments. By investing more aggressively, this type of all-weather fund may offer a greater return, but it also is riskier.

Lifestyle funds, also known as life cycle or life stage funds, are a premixed portfolio of stocks, bonds, and cash. The mixture is based on your age and risk temperament. A lifestyle fund won't be the hottest mutual fund, but it also won't be the coldest.

Some mutual funds bring diversity to your stock portfolio, but that's not the same as asset allocation. For example, a fund of funds is a mutual fund that invests in many other mutual funds. The fund of funds offers greater diversification than a traditional mutual fund. Expenses, however, are likely to be higher, because of the fees charged by the fund of funds and the expenses charged by the underlying funds.

Total stock market index funds give you the diversity of investing in a fund that tracks the Wilshire 5000 index of U.S. stocks that are regularly traded. You don't own foreign stocks if you invest in that index, but you do get a piece of virtually all U.S. stocks. With index funds, you won't beat the market, but you also won't be left behind. The low expenses with index funds increase your chances of doing well.

## REBALANCING YOUR PORTFOLIO

A key element of asset allocation is rebalancing your mixture of investments on a regular basis. You're shifting assets from one class to another, so you have the ideal mix of stocks, bonds, and cash investments.

If you're fortunate and the stocks in your portfolio grow significantly, you might find yourself with too large a percentage of your assets in the stock market. Conversely, if stocks go in the tank, you tend to have too little in equities, so more assets should be shifted to that class. As you rebalance your portfolio in a bear market, you're usually putting more money into the market, rather than running for your life from stock investments.

You're trying to maintain the original equilibrium you had in mind when you established your asset allocation strategy. When one class grows much faster or drops significantly in value, you throw off the equilibrium of your strategy and must rebalance.

Rebalancing often goes against your natural instincts. The end result is that you're frequently taking money out of the investments that are doing well. You're shifting money out of asset classes that have performed exceptionally, because their value is up and they now represent too large a percentage of your investment portfolio. And you're putting the money into asset classes that aren't doing well, because their value now represents too small a percentage of your portfolio.

Market gyrations throw your asset allocation mix off-kilter. For example, when stocks are down significantly, the typical asset allocation formula will show that you have too small a percentage of your assets in the market. Even though your intuition says to stay away from stocks, the asset allocation strategy pushes you to allocate more money into the market.

Sometimes market gyrations will correct your asset allocation mix, but you'll be the loser because of it. For example, many investment advisers suggest that you should only put 5 percent to 10 percent of your stock portfolio in technology companies. When tech stocks had a meltdown, share prices dropped enormously, and you were left with holdings that were 5 percent to 10 percent of your stock portfolio. Unfortunately, that's not how you want to rebalance your portfolio.

Rebalancing might have curbed some of the losses investors sustained in the most recent bear market. Because of skyrocketing stock prices, too much of their money was in equities. Had they rebalanced their portfolio, they would have shifted some of their money to other asset classes like bonds or cash. Although they wouldn't have taken all of their money out of the market, their portfolio would have taken less of a hit during the bear market.

Rebalancing can cause you tax problems if you are selling mutual funds that aren't in a tax-sheltered account. It might be wiser to direct fresh savings toward assets that should make up a larger percentage of your portfolio. Otherwise, if you sell off mutual fund shares as part of your rebalancing, you may create a tax problem for yourself. Taxes aren't a problem if you're rebalancing assets in an IRA, 401(k), or some other tax-sheltered account.

## PROTECTION TIPS

Asset allocation is an extremely important element of your blueprint for protecting and rebuilding your retirement. With the asset allocation strategy, you reduce the risk that every investment in your portfolio will perform badly at the same time. Because your money is spread out among different classes of investments, you haven't put all of your eggs in one basket. Some of your assets may grow, even if others are falling behind.

Even if you're young, some of your money should be in bonds and cash investments. By doing so, you keep your portfolio in balance. If too much of your money is invested in stock, you risk having too much volatility. If too much of your money is in bonds, inflation can eat up your portfolio.

Index funds add diversity to your portfolio and keep your expenses low. Index funds give you the opportunity to tie your fortunes to a broad market index. They have lower expenses than an actively managed fund and are likely to be more tax-efficient.

Rebalancing is counterintuitive, because you're usually funneling more money into an asset class that isn't performing well. The reality, however, is that rebalancing forces you to buy low and sell high, much as your gut tells you otherwise. You should rebalance at least once per year.

Rebalancing can cause tax problems unless you're switching investments in your 401(k) or IRA. Otherwise, you may be paying a great deal more on April 15. A better alternative is to funnel new money into investments that will help to rebalance your portfolio. Another possibility is to limit your rebalancing to tax-sheltered accounts where liquidating investments won't increase your current taxable income.

As you work on your blueprint for protecting and rebuilding your retirement, you'll see quickly if your portfolio is unbalanced. At a minimum, make sure the money you're saving and investing now is used to buy assets that will help balance your portfolio.

# CHAPTER 4

# Protecting your retirement with equity investments

WHEN THE STOCK MARKET WAS BOOMING, MANY PEOPLE THOUGHT THEY could make their living by buying and selling stocks. Day traders buy and sell stocks rapidly to take advantage of fluctuations in the price. They are active traders who buy and sell stocks frequently during the course of a day. At the height of the day-trading phenomenon, young and old people were buying stocks, only to sell the same shares minutes or hours later.

Humorist Andy Borowitz poked fun at these day traders in his book, *The Trillionaire Next Door: The Greedy Investor's Guide to Day Trading.* In his book, Borowitz joked about making the transition from his job assembling Whoppers to earning in the high thirteen figures. His book gives tongue-in-cheek advice to long-term investors, such as which stocks to hold for five, ten, fifteen minutes, or more.

When you're depending upon equity investments to protect your retirement, it's not as easy to laugh about the state of the stock market. Even when you're investing for the long term, it isn't easy watching your investments lose money every day. Furthermore, when the stock market is plummeting, it doesn't seem to matter much if you own conservative or aggressive investments. In either case, you're losing money.

After the stock market chaos of this new century, you may not want to own stock ever again. Although you can protect your retirement without it, you're better off with stock in your portfolio. But you need to be smarter this time around, so you can choose the right equity investments.

## BACK TO BASICS

Stock represents ownership in a company, which is why it's called an equity investment. Equities are generally viewed as a great investment for the long term, but this was not the case if you invested in Enron, World-Com, or a host of Internet stocks that disappeared almost overnight. Even the Sock Puppet couldn't save Pets.com.

Stock is a great way to keep pace with inflation and increase the size of your retirement nest egg. You're not just lending money to someone and receiving interest. You're an owner of the company and share in the profits, as well as the growth of the business.

Dividends are a portion of the company's profits paid out to share-holders. Dividends aren't the same as earnings. Only a portion of the earnings are paid out in dividends. Some profitable companies don't pay out dividends. Instead, they use the money to finance future growth. To calculate the dividend yield, you divide the yearly dividend by the price per share of stock. A fifty-dollar stock that pays out one dollar per year in dividends has an annual dividend yield of 2 percent.

Even if a company doesn't pay a dividend, you hope the shares will go up in value and you can sell them at a profit. Capital gains and losses are the amount you make or lose on the sale of stock. Long-term capital gains are taxed at a lower rate than ordinary income.

While retirees tend to buy dividend-paying stocks for income, divi-dend reinvestment plans are a way for younger investors to build a retirement nest egg over the years. You take those small or large dividend checks and buy more shares with them. There's usually a minimal brokerage fee on each purchase. In addition to your dividend reinvestment, you can also write out a check for twenty-five dollars or much more to buy additional shares. Some dividend reinvestment plans also charge a modest administrative fee.

Dividend reinvestment plans offer a convenient and low-cost way to accumulate shares in a company you think is going to appreciate in value. Whereas the natural tendency is to spend small dividend checks, dividend reinvestment plans automatically invest that money. Assuming the fees are minimal and you intend to buy and hold the stock for years to come, dividend reinvestment plans make a nice forced savings program.

With dividend reinvestment, you need to own one or more shares to get started. You'll need to make your initial purchase of stock through a broker. There are, however, "no-load" stocks that allow you to enroll directly in the company's dividend reinvestment plan, even if you don't own any shares.

**WEBSITES FOR INFORMATION ON DIVIDEND REINVESTMENT AND NO-LOAD STOCKS**

DRIP Central—www.dripcentral.com

DRIP Investor—www.dripinvestor.com

DirectInvesting.com—www.directinvesting.com

## GROWTH VERSUS VALUE INVESTING

If you accept that some of your money needs to be in the stock market to protect your retirement, it helps to distinguish between growth and value investing. They are two different styles of investing. At various times, growth and value investing outperform each other. Even the experts differ on whether you should be buying growth or value stocks. The smart money says you should be buying both for your stock portfolio.

## Investing in growth stocks

When you buy a growth stock, you're hoping the company will become more profitable each year. Although the earnings may grow each year, growth stocks frequently don't pay a dividend or, at best, they pay a small one. Instead of paying dividends to shareholders from the earnings, the company will reinvest most of the profits to trigger even more growth. The belief is that you have to spend money to make money.

Even if a company doesn't pay a dividend, you want to see its earnings increase. The company needs those earnings to finance further expansion. If the price of the stock goes up significantly, shareholders don't care that the company isn't paying a dividend. The increase in value of a stock over and above the price you paid is called capital appreciation.

Growth stocks typically have a high price-to-earnings (P/E) ratio. That means the price is high when compared to earnings. For example, a company that sells for roughly fifty dollars per share, with earnings of about one dollar per share, has a P/E ratio of fifty, and that's high. Some aggressive investors are even willing to buy shares of companies with no earnings.

Make sure you understand the difference between a backward P/E ratio and a forward P/E. The forward P/E is based on predictions of future earnings, not the last four quarters. Those earnings estimates may turn out to be unrealistic.

There are no absolutes when it comes to P/E ratios. During a bear market, the P/E ratio isn't necessarily as reliable as it usually is in evaluating a stock. When the bears are dominating the market, a P/E ratio that used to be attractive may be looked upon with disdain.

When you buy a growth stock, you're betting that the price will continue to go up, even though the earnings don't seem to justify what you're paying now. Growth stocks are sometimes risky, because these companies are often relatively young and may not have a history of being successful through good times and bad.

Even among growth stocks, there are different degrees of risks. A new technology company may be riskier than a growth stock in a different industry with a proven product or service to sell. Also, avoid buying penny stocks. Generally speaking, shares of penny stocks sell for five dollars or less and are extremely risky, because the companies have no history of sales and earnings.

A company that's been around awhile can still be a growth stock. Although they've been around for years, companies like Wal-Mart and McDonald's are still viewed as growth stocks. McDonald's has come under fire in recent months for pushing expansion at the expense of quality and customer service. Wal-Mart has increased growth by expanding its grocery-selling operations.

You'll sometimes see a distinction made between large-cap growth stocks, mid-cap growth stocks, and small-cap growth stocks. The "cap" refers to capitalization. A company's capitalization is calculated by multiplying the number of shares outstanding times the price of one share. A company with a capitalization of under $1 billion is viewed as a small-cap stock.

These smaller companies are viewed as being much more risky than larger ones. On the plus side, however, they have more potential for growth. But, just because a company is poised for growth doesn't mean it actually will move up in value. Predictions of rapid growth, or any growth at all, don't necessarily come to pass.

Growth stocks may be volatile, which means they have wide swings in value. They can soar if rapid growth continues or can plummet if there's bad news, such as a change in management. When you buy a growth stock, you need to think long-term. Your objective should be long-term growth of your money, not a quick profit.

## Investing in value stocks

When you use the strategy of buying value stocks, you hope to find companies that are currently out of favor. Value stocks usually have a low P/E ratio compared to other companies in the same industry. The price you can buy the stock for is low when compared to the company's earnings. Value stocks usually have above-average dividend yields.

Value investors look for stocks that are selling well below their intrinsic value. Typically, the value investor will look at companies in a troubled industry. The P/E ratio of those companies is less than the market average.

The value investor hopes that the troubles with a particular company are temporary in nature. The value investor scouts the marketplace for companies whose stock prices have fallen, but their future still looks bright. The fact that the price per share of a stock has declined does not necessarily mean it is a bargain.

Investors may look at the same stock in a different way. The growth investor may be willing to pay a higher price, because she sees the stock's potential for increased sales and earnings. The value investor, on the other hand, may consider the stock to be overpriced.

Financial services firms often provide lists of stocks appealing to growth and value investors. For example, Schwab Equity Ratings, mentioned earlier, provides lists of large-cap value stocks, large-cap growth stocks, small-cap value stocks, and small-cap growth stocks that are expected to outperform the market.

## DIVIDEND-PAYING STOCKS

Dividend-paying stocks have traditionally been viewed as a relatively safe investment, even during rocky economic times. Dividend-paying stocks, also known as income stocks, are generally viewed as a conservative investment. Stocks that pay dividends tend to hold up better in tough times, but you can't bank on that fact. Shares of dividend-paying stocks will still go down in value during a bear market.

The appeal of dividend-paying stocks is that they're usually quite stable and offer a steady stream of income. As companies mature, they no longer need to plow all of their earnings back into the corporation. Unlike a rapidly growing company, they usually don't need to reinvest all of their profits in new factories or to pay expansion costs. Some of the profits from their business ventures can be returned to investors in the form of dividends.

Dividend-paying stocks tend to be blue-chip companies that have been around for years. Management has demonstrated the ability and willingness to pay dividends out of earnings. A strong company might even be able to pay out regular dividends and still reinvest enough earnings to ensure that growth will continue for years to come.

It might seem like a slam dunk to buy a company that has a long history of paying regular dividends. Often, the dividend is higher than what you would make in a money market fund, and you have the opportunity for capital appreciation as well. In theory, a stock that pays a regular dividend is unlikely to go down too much in value. Nonetheless, it is also less likely to skyrocket in value, and the stockpile might fall if the dividend is slashed.

During the technology boom of the 1990s, investors weren't focused on how much dividend a company paid. They wanted stocks that were growing by the minute, and profits, if any, were plowed back into the company. In the new millennium, stocks that pay dividends are usually a much safer bet, and that has considerable appeal to investors.

Nevertheless, there are risks to consider when buying dividend-paying stocks. The dividend is not guaranteed. The payout won't necessarily last if earnings fall. Dividends are often 50 percent to 75 percent of the company's profits.

It is helpful to look at a company's history of paying dividends. For example, a blue-chip company may have a history of paying dividends in good times and bad. The company's earnings should be continuing to grow, but, there is no guarantee they will.

In fact, dividends at just about any company may shrink due to economic circumstances. The chairman of the H.J. Heinz Co. told shareholders on September 12, 2002, that their dividend checks will get significantly smaller. (Heinz is expected to have lower revenue after spinning off a number of food products to Del Monte.) The shareholders, many of whom were retirees and people on a fixed income, were told to expect the dividend to drop from $1.62 annually to $1.08 per year.

Unless you have a diversified portfolio of dividend-paying stocks, your income will drop significantly when events like this occur. You won't have enough money to buy groceries, either Heinz products or Del Monte.

## MUTUAL FUNDS TO PROTECT YOUR RETIREMENT

As we found out during the long bear market, owning mutual funds run by brilliant fund managers doesn't mean you'll make money. Although a mutual fund helps to diversify your portfolio, it is no assurance that your investments will stay afloat during troubled economic times. When the entire market is a disaster, it won't matter much if you're invested in a quality mutual fund that's run by experienced professionals.

The professionals seem to be every bit as helpless as the rest of us during a prolonged bear market. That's why you should be investing in several mutual funds with different investment objectives. Owning different mutual funds with varying investment objectives gives you diversity you won't get by owning one fund. Mutual funds also make it easy to invest and withdraw money automatically.

To protect your retirement, don't allow your investment to be eaten away by fees and sales commissions. Author Andrew Tobias calls these expenses the "weight of the jockey." These expenses weigh down your investment's performance like an overweight jockey slows down a horse.

The load, which is a commission or sales charge, really weighs down that horse. A true no-load mutual fund charges no front-end or back-end sales commission. A front-end load is deducted from your original investment to pay the broker. If you invest $100 and the front-end load is 5 percent, only ninety-five dollars is invested.

A back-end load is also known as a deferred sales charge. There is no sales commission when you invest initially, but you're charged if you leave the fund within a specified period of time, usually five years. In some instances, the back-end load is reduced for each year that you keep your money invested.

Other funds apply a 12b-1 fee that is a charge for marketing expenses and distribution. The 12b-1 fee is an indirect way of compensating the broker who sold the fund. Even though the 12b-1 fee will be less than one percent, it cuts into the return on your investment.

As mentioned earlier, the mutual fund company that doesn't charge a load makes its money on annual fees. The expense ratio of a mutual fund is a percentage of the mutual fund's total assets.

Fees are spelled out in the prospectus. The prospectus is a legal document that explains a mutual fund's investment objectives, risks, financial highlights, and fees. As mentioned earlier, index funds normally have much lower expenses than actively managed funds.

If you're serious about protecting your retirement, you need to read the prospectus and see what risks you're taking with your money. The prospectus states the fund's investment objectives and what strategy the portfolio manager will utilize to reach those objectives. Make sure the investment objectives in the prospectus match your own. Look for red flags like pending lawsuits.

## ANALYZING THE PROSPECTUS

When you review the prospectus, pay particular attention to these items:

Overview—What the fund's purpose is and how your money will be invested

Objectives, Strategies, and Risks—Detailed information that helps you see if the fund's strategy coincides with your risk tolerance and time horizon (it tells you how investments for the fund are chosen).

Fund Performance History—How volatile the fund has been

Fees and Expenses—The fees and expenses you're paying

Management—Who's managing your money

Share Price and Distributions/Taxes—What taxes to expect

## MUTUAL FUNDS FOR CONSERVATIVE INVESTORS

During a bear market, there are few pure stock mutual funds that will protect you. All of them are likely to be down in value. Nevertheless, some stock mutual funds are less volatile than others. They will go down during tough economic times, but usually not as much as riskier mutual funds. Conversely, they probably won't go up as much during a bull market.

We looked above at dividend-paying stocks and income stocks. When you buy these stocks, you're getting a company with a history of paying regular dividends. If you want someone else to pick which companies to buy, you can purchase shares in a mutual fund that invests in stocks that pay regular dividends. Mutual funds with this investment objective are often called equity income or dividend funds.

Don't confuse an equity income fund, which invests in stocks that pay high dividends, with an income fund. Income funds invest primarily in bonds, which are debts owed by a corporation or the federal government (or one of its agencies).

To further muddy the water, there are growth-and-income funds. The managers of these funds seek out capital growth and income for shareholders. You'll need to look at the growth-and-income fund's prospectus to figure out the fund manager's strategy for achieving this objective. Some managers are required to invest a significant percentage of the fund's assets in income-producing securities such as bonds, as well as dividend-paying stocks. Some growth-and-income fund managers invest in growth stocks that pay little or no dividends, as well as income stocks that pay high dividends.

## UTILITIES

Utilities used to be a prime example of conservative, dividend-paying stocks. Companies in the utilities sector provide basic services like water, gas, electricity, and telephone service. Before deregulation, you could count on these companies being profitable, since every home needs these services. You could bank on regular dividends, even in a recession. Deregulation ended utility companies' legal monopoly.

Utilities used to be an investment that was safe enough for widows and orphans. During the tech stock boom, however, many utilities decided they wanted more out of life. Because of deregulation, they were able to move into many new enterprises. Many utilities faltered as they moved into new businesses. The utilities sector, which used to be one of the safest, is now one of the riskiest.

Despite the problems suffered by a number of high-profile utility stocks, there are solid utilities with a history of paying high dividends. To protect your retirement, you may want to have a small portion of your portfolio in utility stocks. Nevertheless, they're not recession-proof and may be risky.

Because of the increased risk associated with utility stocks, some mutual fund companies are abandoning their utility stock funds. They are replacing their utility stock funds with funds that focus on dividend-paying companies. The equity income fund you invest in might have a percentage of its assets in utility stocks.

## PRINCIPAL PROTECTED FUNDS

Even though a company invests in solid, dividend-paying companies, there is no guarantee that you'll avoid losing money. There are, however, mutual funds that guarantee you won't lose the capital you've invested. These investments go by many names, including principal protected funds. You'll also see them called target maturity, capital preservation, or guaranteed mutual funds.

As the names suggest, the primary objective of these funds is to ensure that your principal remains intact. The fund manager also shoots for a modest gain on the money invested. Principal protected funds add a measure of safety to your portfolio.

Some principal protected funds carry insurance to make sure you won't lose principal. Others keep a significant amount of their portfolio in bonds. This cuts into the fund's earnings, since stocks usually make more than bonds in the long run.

On large mutual fund company uses zero coupon Treasury bonds to guarantee the principal of its target maturity funds. Zero coupon bonds are purchased at a discount from face value. When it matures, the zero coupon bond is redeemed at its face value. The fund manager buys enough zero coupon bonds to guarantee the return of the investor's principal. The target maturity fund investor must reinvest all dividends and hold shares to their maturity in order to take advantage of the principal guarantee.

The sales and management fees with principal protected funds are often higher than those associated with other mutual funds. Unless you hold the shares for the required period, you may be penalized when shares are liquidated.

Over an extended period, investors might achieve the same results or better with a conservative balanced fund that is a mixture of stocks and bonds. There are no insurance components and lower fees. On the other hand, there are also no guarantees that the principal will remain intact.

## USING RATING SERVICES TO EVALUATE MUTUAL FUNDS

There are many rating services that can help you decide which mutual fund to choose. The Morningstar rating helps investors decide which funds to include in their portfolios. Morningstar (www.morningstar.com) is an investment research firm that provides ratings of mutual funds. The firm separates funds in forty narrowly defined categories. The fund gives a star rating based on performance.

Unfortunately, past history is no guarantee of future performance or that you'll make money on your investment. The Morningstar rating is just one of many factors investors should consider in deciding which fund to buy. You should also consider whether the fund's investment approach is compatible with your investment goals, time horizon, and risk tolerance.

A Morningstar analyst recently issued a report warning investors about sector funds. The sector fund manager buy shares of companies in a specific economic sector such as financial services, real estate, healthcare, defense, and technology. The Morningstar analyst found that sector fund investors earned an average annual return that was much lower than investors in diversified funds. The investor in a sector fund tends to be drawn in by spectacular gains, but the sector is often on its way down rather than up.

Lipper is also in the business of evaluating mutual funds. Its new rating system, Lipper Leaders, can help you narrow down your choices. Their website is www.lipperweb.com.

## PROTECTION TIPS

The blueprints for a house are just the beginning of the building process. You may want to move in tomorrow, but you can't rush the process. Similarly, you can't bank on aggressive investing to speed up your plans for retirement. When you do have large investment gains, you need to take some money off the table. You need to save more aggressively, rather than putting all of your money on one long shot.

The stock market is the best way to build wealth over the long run. Other investments help you maintain wealth and may keep pace with inflation, but buying stock in quality companies helps you build the size of your nest egg.

In the past few years, many experts thought the stock market had reached the bottom and advised investors to jump back in with both feet. Unfortunately, the market hadn't reached the bottom. Timing the stock market is a bad strategy for investors hoping to protect and rebuild their retirement.

You also can't time when growth or value investing will produce the best results. Therefore, you need to own quality growth and value stocks in your portfolio.

Many experts believe that dividends are one of the most important factors in deciding which stocks to buy. They are the driving force behind a stock's increase in value. Dividends are an important measure of a company's profitability.

Chasing the hot mutual fund is not the answer to protecting and rebuilding your retirement. You need to develop a long-term strategy for investing, even if you're well along in years. Before investing, make sure you read the mutual fund's prospectus. The prospectus is a legal document that gives you the scoop on how your money will be invested. By keeping five to seven years of living expenses in liquid investments, you can avoid selling mutual fund shares during rocky times.

# CHAPTER 5

# Protecting your retirement with income investments

During a bear market, investors are like compulsive gamblers. They pledge to God that if they can just break even, they'll take all of their money out of the stock market. Unfortunately, like the gambler who never breaks even, some stocks will never return to their previous values, no matter how long you hold on to them.

When you're losing thousands of dollars in the stock market, breaking even looks awfully good. Income investments are often criticized as barely keeping up with inflation, but that doesn't seem so bad when your stock portfolio is cut in half. Carl Tannenbaum, chief economist with LaSalle Bank, was quoted by the Associated Press as saying, "Sometimes it is not the return on principal but the return of principal." Tannenbaum went on to say, "Never discount the value of having stodgier things in your portfolio."

Retirees, and many people planning for retirement, have been burned by the stock market. If you're among them, you may be looking for safer alternatives like income investments. Your goal is to increase your income without increasing your risk of loss.

## CONSERVATIVE INVESTMENTS

Even the most conservative investments have some degree of risk. The most obvious risk is that the return on those investments will not keep up with inflation and you will be losing purchasing power each day. The $100 you invest today may not buy nearly as much a year from now. Taxes will also eat away at the meager return on your investment.

Some of the most conservative investments can be found at your local bank or savings and loan. The infamous passbook savings account pays very little interest, but is extremely safe. Your bank may offer a money market account that pays a low interest rate. Often, the interest on these accounts is based on how much you've deposited. Larger accounts pay a higher rate of interest.

Conservative investors who want safety and income love the sound of CDs. The certificate of deposit (CD) is an investment where the investor receives a fixed rate of return on funds that are deposited for a specified length of time. CDs are issued by banks, savings and loans, and credit unions. The typical CD is insured by the FDIC or the FSLIC and there is usually a penalty for early withdrawal.

FDIC coverage is normally $100,000 per ownership category at that particular bank. Retirement accounts are insured separately from other accounts you may have at the same bank. For specific questions, call the FDIC at 800-934-3342 or check its website, which can be found at www.fdic.gov.

CD investors must often commit to a longer term to get a higher interest rate. This type of trade-off is tough to make when CDs are paying in the neighborhood of 3 percent. If you don't want to be locked in too much, you can "ladder" the maturity dates of your CDs so they come due at regular intervals.

Laddering works like this: If you have $10,000 to invest, you might put $2,000 in a six-month CD. You might buy another $2,000 CD that matures in one year. With the remaining $6,000, you can stagger the maturity dates so they come due on a regular basis. If interest rates rise, you can commit to a longer term. Laddering also helps you to avoid having to cash in a CD prematurely and paying a penalty.

Be wary of callable CDs. This provision in your investment contract allows the financial institution to end the agreement after a specified number of months or years. The financial institution will exploit this feature if interest rates go down significantly and it feels the interest rate being paid is too high.

You should be willing to shop around for the best rate on your CDs. Banks are always offering promotional rates on CDs. Furthermore, many are willing to give you a higher rate to match that of a competitor or to keep a good customer. Check Bankrate.com (www.bankrate.com) and Banxquote (www.banx.com) for interest rates across the country. Credit unions sometimes pay higher rates on CDs, so check out www.cuna.org to see if you're eligible to join one or call 1-800-358-5710.

After you've bought a CD, don't get lazy when it comes up for renewal. You need to shop around for the best rate each time it comes up for renewal. Don't assume you're getting the best rate, even though it's easy and painless to roll over the CD for another term.

Finally, don't assume your favorite bank employee has your best interest at heart. When customers complain about low interest rates, bank employees are taught to push other bank products like annuities and mutual funds. Even if those products are right for you, the ones offered by your bank may not be ideal. They are also not insured by the FDIC.

## MONEY MARKET FUNDS

Money market funds offered by a mutual fund company are a good parking place for your money, but they won't generate much income when interest rates are low. Money market funds do, however, give you ready access to your cash when you need it. They often, but not always, offer a slightly higher yield than passbook savings accounts, and you don't need to tie up your money.

Money market funds invest primarily in short-term debt instruments that are of the highest quality, such as Treasury bills. It is almost impossible to lose part of your principal in a money market fund. Nevertheless, they are not as safe as the money market accounts, savings accounts, and CDs you get at a bank, nor are they insured by the FDIC.

Money market funds do not provide the opportunity for capital appreciation. Their emphasis is on safety, stability, and liquidity. As a result, their performance is likely to pale in comparison to stocks and bonds over the long haul. Of course, it's extremely unlikely you'll ever have a negative return as you will occasionally with stocks and bonds.

Some money market funds don't perform as well as others. The fund manager makes decisions each day that might improve the yield or cause it to lag in comparison to other funds. Some money market funds take greater risks in an attempt to increase the yield. Though losing any of your principal is unlikely, a money market fund is not insured by the FDIC. Companies like iMoneyNet (www.imoneynet.com) track money market yields.

Even if you ladder your CDs, you still may not have your money exactly when you need it. Money market funds give you access to your money whenever you need it. They're a great place to keep funds for an emergency. Money market funds are a great parking place for cash you'll need for a wedding, down payment on a home, college expenses, or some other purpose.

## BACK TO BASICS

When you buy a bond of any kind, you're lending money, and interest is paid to you. Bonds are an IOU to the investor from whoever issued them. Bonds are considered to be a debt investment. A bond is actually a loan that investors make to a corporation or the government that pays a stated return over a specified period of time.

There are two broad categories of bonds to invest in: government bonds and corporate bonds. A government bond is typically issued by some branch of government, whether it be federal, state, or local. Corporate bonds are issued because companies don't always borrow from banks and often use bonds to raise money.

With either type of bond, the issuer agrees to pay a specified interest rate. Usually, this interest is paid semiannually. The issuer also promises to give back the total amount borrowed when the bond matures. The total amount borrowed is the face value of the bond.

The interest paid out on a bond usually depends upon the economic climate at the time it's issued and the safety of the investment. When you buy a bond issued by the U.S. government, you can be absolutely sure your interest and the amount borrowed will be paid on time. Corporate bonds pay a higher interest rate but your investment isn't as secure.

Companies with financial troubles must pay a higher interest rate to attract investors for their bonds. These investors take the risk that the company will not make interest payments at the appropriate time and the amount borrowed may never be paid back. Junk bonds are issued by companies that may not be able to pay back what they owe.

Investors can buy a bond when it's first issued or in the secondary market. Bonds that have not yet matured are bought and sold in the secondary market. The price of a bond in the secondary market depends upon how much interest it pays and how that interest rate compares to bonds that are being issued for the first time.

Bond prices in the secondary market move in the opposite direction of interest rates. For example, if interest rates are falling, bond prices move up. If interest rates are rising, bond prices fall.

Suppose you own a $10,000 bond paying 5 percent that won't mature for a long while. If the interest rate of a comparable newly issued bond is less than 5 percent, your $10,000 bond will sell at a premium, which means you'll get more than the face amount. If that 5 percent doesn't look so good because interest rates are up, your $10,000 bond will sell at a discount, which means you'll get less than the face amount.

Rising or falling interest rates aren't the only factor that affects the price of a bond. If the word gets out that a corporation or municipality is having financial problems, no one may want to buy its bonds. In addition, much like the callable CD we looked at earlier, some bonds allow the issuer to call or redeem them before maturity, which means the investor won't necessarily enjoy a high interest rate for as long as anticipated.

Bonds are usually viewed as a conservative investment. Older investors often keep bonds in their portfolio as a source of income and a less-risky alternative to the stock market.

Bonds are not risk-free, even if you hold them until maturity. The interest rate you're getting might not keep up with inflation. Furthermore, your original investment that you get back at maturity might not buy as much due to inflation. Down the road, the face value of the bond won't have the same purchasing power as it does now. Furthermore, if the interest from bonds is your only income, your standard of living will suffer as consumer prices rise.

## RISKY BOND BUSINESS

Despite their stodgy reputation, bonds are anything but risk-free. There is a credit risk with certain bonds. The entity responsible for paying you interest and your principal at maturity may run into financial problems. Martin D. Weiss, chairman of Weiss Ratings, Inc., in Palm Beach Gardens, Florida, said in the September 15, 2002, issue of *Bottom Line Personal* that corporate bonds are too risky for most investors. According to Weiss, the soft economy and financial scandals have damaged the credit quality of many bonds.

Certain bonds are better than others in protecting your retirement. Here are some of your choices:

### Treasury Securities

- Treasury securities are the safest investment you can get. Treasury bills are short-term government securities with maturity dates of no more than one year. They're also called T-bills. Treasury notes mature in more than one year but no longer than ten years from their date of issue. Treasury bonds are longer-term securities of ten years or more, but the Treasury Department hasn't issued a bond since October 2001. At that time, it suspended issuance of the thirty-year bond. Savings bonds are not the same as Treasury bonds, even though they are issued by the Treasury Department. Savings bonds cannot be bought and sold on the open market.

## Corporate Bonds

- With corporate bonds, you are lending money to a corporation. Because they are not backed by the full faith and credit of the government, they pay a higher interest rate than U.S. Treasury securities. Just as individuals have different credit ratings, corporations are viewed as having varying degrees of credit-worthiness. The bonds of financially secure corporations are investment-grade and pay less interest than the bonds of companies whose ability to repay is suspect. Lower-quality bonds, sometimes called junk bonds, pay a higher yield, but pose a greater risk of default.

## Municipal Bonds

- A municipal bond is an IOU from a state, city, school district, or public entity. Though they pay less interest than a corporate bond, you save on federal income taxes unless you're subject to the alternative minimum tax. They're exempt from state and local taxes if the issuer is in your state of residence. You can buy municipal bonds that are insured by large companies like MBIA Insurance Company and Ambac Assurance Corporation.

## Zero Coupon Bonds

- Zero coupon bonds are issued at a discount and increase in value until reaching maturity. Although interest is not paid out to the bondholder, you pay taxes on the income as if it were.

## TREASURYS

If protecting your income is your top priority and you have an extremely low tolerance for risk, Treasury securities may be the right choice for you.

To borrow money from the public, the U.S. Treasury issues bills and notes. The federal government guarantees the principal and interest. The interest is taxable, but you won't pay state or local taxes. Treasury bills and notes can be sold on the secondary market.

As mentioned above, Treasury bills are known as T-bills and mature in one year or less from the date of issue. You buy a T-bill for less than its face (par) value. At maturity, the Treasury pays the face value. Your interest is the difference between what you paid for the T-bill and its face value.

## Treasury inflation-protected securities (TIPS)

The Treasury sells fixed-principal and inflation-indexed securities. Treasury Inflation-Protected Securities (TIPS), also known as Treasury Inflation-Indexed Securities, are becoming increasingly popular. The Bureau of the Public Debt refers to TIPS as the "safest of the safest investments" (www.publicdebt.treas.gov). They're backed by the U.S. government, and their ultimate value can't be diminished by inflation.

With inflation-indexed securities, the principal is adjusted semiannually based on changes in the Consumer Price Index, but the annual interest rate stays the same. The interest is paid every six months. At maturity, you receive the face value of the security. The downside with inflation-indexed securities is that you pay income taxes every year on the interest, as well as the step-up in value of the security's principal. This is a good reason to buy these securities in a tax-sheltered account.

Researchers for Ibbotson Associates, a leading authority on asset allocation, recommended that TIPS be viewed as a separate and distinct asset class. According to these researchers, TIPS possess unique characteristics that you won't find in most investment vehicles. TIPS provide a direct hedge against one specific measure of inflation and offer significant diversification benefits.

The Treasury holds about 150 auctions each year. Two-year notes are auctioned monthly. Five- and ten-year notes are auctioned on a quarterly basis. In January, July, and October, the Treasury offers inflation-indexed ten-year notes. Large investors bid competitively for the securities. You'll get the yield set by the auction.

You can purchase the bills and notes directly from the government through an electronic service called TreasuryDirect (www.treasurydirect .gov; 1-800-722-2678). The minimum purchase is $1,000, and additional purchases must be in multiples of $1,000. You can also buy the bills and notes from banks, brokerage firms, and Federal Reserve banks. Private firms normally charge a fee or a commission.

## SAVINGS BONDS

Savings bonds are an extremely conservative investment. Although they pay a relatively low interest rate, savings bonds offer tax advantages that will be discussed in detail in Chapter 14. In view of the stock market's roller coaster ride of the past few years, savings bonds may look more appealing. Although they are issued by the U.S. Treasury, they do not trade in the secondary market like other Treasury products.

Series HH bonds pay out income twice per year and are only available in exchange for other bonds. The biggest advantage with HH bonds is that they allow you to continue deferring interest accumulated on your old Series E, EE, Savings Notes, and H bonds. Bonds may be converted up to a year after their final maturity.

I bonds are a relatively new product issued by the Treasury. The return on the bond is linked to an inflation index. There is a fixed rate assigned at purchase, which remains with the bond for life. In addition, a portion of the bond's earnings are tied to the Consumer Price Index and offers protection against inflation.

Unlike the older series E and series EE bonds, the I bond is purchased at face value. Upon redemption, the bond owner receives the face value of the bond, plus all of the interest that has accrued. The I bond increases in value monthly, and interest is compounded semiannually.

I bonds purchased after February 3, 2003, must be held for at least twelve months before cashing. But if you don't hold it for five years, you lose three months' worth of interest. The bond has a thirty-year life span before it stops earning interest.

You can buy EE and I bonds through most financial institutions. A better idea is to buy bonds directly from the U.S. Department of the Treasury. You may even use a credit card to make the purchase, preferably one that gives you a cash rebate or frequent flyer miles. Make sure you pay your credit card bill in full or you'll pay more in finance charges than you're earning on your bonds. The Treasury allows $15,000 in EE bond purchases each calendar year and $30,000 in I bonds.

More information, as well as calculators, are available on the Internet at www.savingsbond.gov and www.publicdebt.treas.gov. The foremost authority on savings bonds is Daniel Pederson, president of Savings Bond Informer, Inc. His website is www.bondhelp.com. Information is also available at www.savingsbond.com. These websites can tell you which of your bonds have reached their final maturity and are no longer paying interest.

## DECIDING WHICH BONDS TO BUY

Just as your bank won't lend you a dime until it sees your credit rating, you shouldn't buy a bond until you see the credit rating of the company offering it. One well-respected rating service is Moody's (www.moodys.com). Moody's top rating is AAA, but few companies these days earn that top grade. Just one company, GE, has held the top grade from Moody's since 1960. Fewer than ten companies have the AAA rating right now. Baa or higher is considered to be investment-grade.

A second major rating service is Standard & Poor's (www.standardandpoors.com). Its top rating is AAA. A bond with a BBB or higher rating is classified as investment-grade.

In addition to the credit rating of the company, investors also look at the yield. The yield is guaranteed if the bond is held to maturity.

To mitigate the risk of rising interest rates, an investor can hold the bond to maturity. The investor can buy bonds with varying maturities, so cash will be available at regular intervals. For example, the investor might buy bonds maturing in two, four, six, eight, and ten years. This strategy is also referred to as laddering.

We discussed laddering previously in conjunction with CDs. You make sure your CDs come due at regular intervals, so cash is available on an ongoing basis. When you ladder bonds, you arrange for them to mature on a regular basis and create an ongoing source of cash. You're also able to reinvest the money and take advantage of higher interest rates.

Traditionally, you needed a minimum investment of $5,000 to $25,000 to buy bonds. Small investors can now buy individual bonds for as little as $1,000. There are no hidden fees or markups to cover the broker's sales commission. You go through a bond wholesaler such as Incapital (1-800-289-6689; www.internotes.com) or LaSalle Broker Dealer Services division (1-877-373-0322; www.directnotes.com).

## BOND MUTUAL FUNDS

If buying individual bonds isn't your cup of tea, you might consider buying a bond mutual fund. A bond mutual fund is professionally managed and gives you a diversified portfolio. The prospectus tells you what bonds are held by the fund and the amount of risk you're taking with your investment. The fund manager decides which bonds to buy and sell. The parameters for these buy-and-sell decisions must be in compliance with the fund's investment objective, which can be found in the prospectus.

You can sell your shares in the bond mutual fund at any time, but you'll receive the net asset value (NAV) for each share. NAV reflects the actual value of each bond in the fund's portfolio. NAV is recalculated on a daily basis and may be higher or lower than the amount you paid per share.

Bond mutual funds are quite appealing to passive investors, but they aren't risk-free. Although bond mutual funds are considered to be fixed income investments, the value of your shares go up and down. If interest rates in general are going up, the odds are good that the value of your shares will go down. That's especially dangerous when interest rates are near record lows. The odds are good that when interest rates do rise, and they eventually will, the value of bonds held by the fund will go down.

Short-term bond funds will have milder price fluctuations due to interest rates. Short-term usually means a maturity date of three years or less. If you invest in intermediate or long-term bond funds, share prices are much more likely to fluctuate in response to the rise and fall of interest rates.

Bond funds come in many categories and offer distinct advantages over buying an individual bond. You can buy shares for a relatively small amount. You can arrange for the fund to send you a check each month. You can reduce your risk when purchasing high-yield junk bonds because the fund owns many different issues, all of which were purchased by a fund manager who knows far more than you ever will about the risk of the issuer defaulting.

Unfortunately, you take the good with the bad when you invest in bond funds. The annual management expenses of a fund, which may be 0.80 percent or more, reduce your yield. With individual bonds, you can lock in an income stream. With a bond fund, assuming you only want the interest paid out to you, your monthly income may fluctuate because of rising and falling rates.

When you're buying a bond fund, you need to focus on the total return, which is the yield, plus or minus any increase or reduction in the price of the bonds. If interest rates go up and the value of bonds in the fund's portfolio go down, you might lose more than you're making in interest. A financial website like Morningstar.com compares a bond fund's yield with its total return.

## BOND FUND CHOICES

The classification of a bond mutual fund is based upon the type of bonds it purchases. Often categories overlap, and the fund manager purchases a mixture of bonds, such as corporate and government bonds.

### Income bond funds

Income bond funds typically invest in a mixture of corporate and government bonds. U.S. government income funds invest in variety of government obligations such as U.S. Treasury securities, Ginnie Maes, and other government notes. Even when a bond invests in government obligations, there is still a significant risk that the fund's shares will go way down in value as interest rates rise.

## Corporate bond funds

Corporate bond funds primarily invest in bonds issued by corporations. The portfolio may be rounded out with U.S. Treasury securities or bonds issued by a federal agency. The prospectus will tell you what types of bonds are being purchased. (The fund manager will usually stick with investment-grade corporate bonds.)

## High-yield bond funds

High-yield bond funds invest in bonds that are issued by companies who may not be around to make good on your investment. Instead of investment-grade bonds, you're most likely investing in junk bonds. To compensate you for the risk you're taking, these bonds pay a higher interest rate. Some high-yield bond funds also invest in convertible securities and preferred stock.

## Ginnie Mae funds

Ginnie Maes are bonds backed by the Government National Mortgage Association (GNMA). The money invested in these bonds is used to make home mortgages. You're paid from the principal and interest payments made by these homeowners.

The U.S. government guarantees the payment if the homeowner defaults on the mortgage. Though the mortgages are backed by the government, the bonds in the portfolio will go down if interest rates rise. Therefore, the value of your shares in the fund will go down if interest rates rise.

## Municipal bond funds

When you invest in a municipal bond fund, your investment buys you a portfolio of bonds issued by states, cities, school districts, and municipalities. The yield is relatively low, but you don't share your payout with the IRS. For instance, if you're in the 30 percent tax bracket, a 1.3 percent tax-free yield is equal to 1.86 percent before federal income taxes. The payout from the fund may also be exempt from state and local taxes.

You'll find several categories of municipal bond funds. As an example, short-term municipal bond funds buy bonds that mature in a relatively short period of time.

## Index bond funds

There are index bond funds that purchase a shopping basket full of bonds. For example, the Total Bond Market Index Fund from Vanguard tracks the taxable bond market. Another possibility is an index fund that tracks the municipal bond market. Even though your index bond fund portfolio is filled with every kind of bond and you're well-diversified, share prices are still likely to go down when interest rates rise.

## BONDS VERSUS BOND MUTUAL FUNDS

A writer posed a simple question in the August 5, 2002, edition of *The Spear Report*, an investment newsletter. The question was, "What should my Mom buy so she can have a safe and reliable monthly income from her life savings?" The writer's 78-year-old mother is very conservative and is still ticked off at having lost $600 in the tech stock debacle.

The writer gave a simplistic answer, but it contained a good deal of useful information. He advised Mom to stay away from bond funds, because you only own shares in the fund, not the bonds themselves. You're exposed to the inverse relationship between interest rates and bond prices. If interest rates are low, the fund's total return will go down as rates go up. When interest rates rise, Mom will lose principal. The writer was also concerned that the bond fund's portfolio might include the next Enron, Adelphia Communications, Global Crossing, United Airlines, or WorldCom.

The writer suggested that Mom buy high-quality corporate bonds. It's simpler, he suggested, to buy new bonds rather than those available on the secondary market. You can find new bonds at your local discount brokerage firm, and there are new ones available each week. The bonds are priced to include broker fees. If the corporation issuing the bond goes bankrupt, bond holders get paid back before common stock holders.

Nevertheless, buying individual bonds isn't necessarily the answer for people interested in protecting their retirement. Sure, you can hold the bond until maturity and not lose principal, but you are losing purchasing power. The $1,000 that you invest today, as well as the interest checks, won't buy nearly as much ten years from now.

The writer's Mom might want to consider ultra short-term bond funds, especially if interest rates are low and are likely to go up. These short-term bond funds invest in high-quality government and corporate securities. The average maturity date of the bonds held by the fund is slightly longer than money market funds, but short enough to curb the risk of loss to principal if interest rates rise. The average maturities range from one to three years.

Intermediate-term bond funds hold securities with longer maturities and offer a higher interest rate. The average maturity in intermediate-term bond funds might range from three to seven years. If interest rates rise, the investor is likely to lose principal. One rule of thumb is that the intermediate-term bond fund loses about 5 percent in value for each 1 percent rise in interest rates. You might question whether it's worth the risk of losing principal to get a higher interest rate.

To avoid taxes, you might opt for municipal bond funds. Although payouts are lower, you won't pay taxes. You have your choice of short-term, intermediate-term, and long-term municipal bond funds.

## CONVERTIBLE CORPORATE BONDS

One of the big knocks on bonds is that inflation erodes your buying power, and your investment doesn't grow like stock does. A compromise approach is to buy convertible corporate bonds.

Convertible bonds can be exchanged for the issuer's common stock. The convertible bond pays a decent interest rate, though not as much as a regular bond from that company. If the company's stock flourishes, the bond can be converted into stock.

Convertible bonds are sensitive to fluctuations in interest rates, but not as much as conventional bonds. Often, convertible bonds are issued by less than solid companies. Usually, the yield on a convertible bond is more than the dividend on the company's stock.

Since convertible bonds are tough to select, you might consider a convertible bond fund. The fund manager selects the bonds. There are many no-load convertible bond funds.

## PROTECTION TIPS

Although income investments should be included in your blueprint for protecting and rebuilding your retirement, you can't rest your financial future on that foundation alone. Bonds, which are generally viewed as a safe investment for retirees, are not risk-free. Inflation eats away at the value of bonds and the interest they pay. You also are at risk if you want to sell your bonds before the maturity date. The value fluctuates in relation to interest rates. You can lose more in principal than you might gain in interest.

In contrast to individual bonds, bond funds never mature, and there is a greater risk of losing principal when interest rates rise. Bond funds may wind up with periods of negative total returns. To lower the volatility of bond funds, stick with a fund that invests in short-term or intermediate-term bonds. In addition, stay away from high-yield or junk bonds, which carry a greater risk of the issuer defaulting.

A bond fund gives you a great deal of diversification. You'll get even more diversification with a bond index fund. The bond index fund has a shopping basket filled with bonds. The bond index fund is likely to have lower expenses. Shoot for a fund where the expense ratio is less than 0.5 percent per year. Even if you're relatively young, some of your money should be in bonds to keep your portfolio in balance.

U.S. Treasury securities that mature in five years or less can help to protect your portfolio. Even if you buy inflation-indexed Treasury securities, however, you may not have enough to live on without investing more aggressively. The yield on those securities won't necessarily provide enough income to help you thrive in retirement.

Keeping up with inflation isn't enough to protect your retirement. As you age, some of your portfolio should be invested for growth, and that means having a percentage of your assets in the stock market.

Even if you're too frightened to invest in anything other than bank CDs, shop around for the best interest rate. The bank across the street may give you a better rate, especially if you're a good customer. Don't hesitate to tell the bank employee what promotions are going on elsewhere and see if the bank will match or beat that rate. Consolidate your accounts and CDs to take advantage of higher interest rates on larger balances.

# CHAPTER 6

# Protecting your retirement
# with annuities

On August 4, 2002, *The Wall Street Journal* Sunday edition printed readers' reaction to the market downturn and how they have been affected by the turmoil. A woman from Boca Raton, Florida, wrote that her variable annuity lost 35 percent in value. She switched to a fixed annuity and is living on the monthly income, along with a small amount of Social Security. Although the woman's accountant advised against the switch, she described her emotional relief as "unmeasurable."

Over the years, annuities have provided the same emotional relief for many retirees. But as this Florida woman found out, annuities come in all forms and offer different levels of protection. Since this woman had no other investments to speak of, a variable annuity may have been the wrong choice. You need to understand the basics, so you can decide if an annuity is right for you and which kind fits your circumstances.

After the helter-skelter market of the early 2000s, annuities will get more attention as a way to protect your retirement. When you buy an annuity, you can create a lifetime stream of income for yourself, a spouse, a child, or some other person. If you make the right choices, you can make sure you'll have enough money to live on for the rest of your life.

## BACK TO BASICS

Mary Beth Franklin of *Kiplinger's* has called annuities "do-it-yourself-pensions." When you buy an annuity, you sign a contract with an insurance company. You give them money now, so they'll pay you money later. You can invest a few thousand dollars or as much as you want. The insurance company expects to earn more on your money than it will pay out. In addition, mortality and expense charges are built into the cost of the annuity.

With an annuity, it's important to distinguish between the accumulation phase and the payout phase. The accumulation phase is the period of time during which your annuity grows in value. After the accumulation phase is over, you can convert the value of the annuity into a stream of income.

When you invest in an immediate annuity, you're skipping the accumulation phase. The money you're depositing is converted immediately into an income stream for an agreed-upon length of time. Your lump sum payment to the insurance company is used to create a lifetime income or some other agreed-upon payout.

While immediate annuities are used to generate income, deferred annuities are designed to build retirement savings. With the deferred annuity, you make a series of contributions or a lump sum deposit. During the tax-deferred accumulation phase, the money grows until you're ready to start enjoying the money from that annuity. Usually, you need to be age 59½ or older to avoid paying a 10 percent penalty on earnings that are distributed.

With the single premium deferred annuity, you invest a lump sum, and the tax-deferred earnings on that payment grow over the years. When you're ready to retire, you look at your financial situation and choose a payout option that will hopefully meet your needs. Your payout is normally a combination of earnings and principal. Assuming you're at least 59½, you'll only be taxed on the earnings withdrawn.

## Fixed versus variable annuities

As the woman from Boca Raton found out, there are two basic types of annuities: fixed and variable. The danger with having a fixed annuity is that the rate is typically guaranteed for a limited amount of time, perhaps one year. Companies sometimes offer teaser rates and first-year bonuses that make it appear as if you're getting a better rate on the annuity, but they're only temporary.

If the rate goes down, you're usually stuck with that annuity for five to ten years unless you pay a surrender charge. The surrender charge is the penalty you pay for switching to another insurance company's annuity or cashing in your annuity too soon after buying it. A typical surrender charge is 7 percent, and goes down a percentage point each year until it disappears entirely.

When interest rates are low and the stock market is soaring, variable annuities are easy to love. Variable annuities offer a number of investment options, and you decide how your money is invested, not the insurance company. Many variable annuity investors spread their money among stock mutual funds. These investment options have varying degrees of risk.

Along with the risks, variable annuities usually have significant fees and expenses. In addition to the premiums for insurance, you're paying mutual fund management fees that may be quite steep.

Variable annuities guarantee that if you die before beginning to take out money, you receive as much as you put in, even if you've lost money. New variable annuities often guarantee a specified rate of return, plus what you've put in. Some variable annuities will even let you lock in your investment gains. Keep in mind, however, that you'll pay higher charges to add these guarantees.

One nice feature with variable annuities is that you can easily switch investments without causing yourself a tax problem. You're taxed when you withdraw earnings from the annuity, not when you sell shares and put them elsewhere in the variable annuity. When it's time to receive payments from the variable annuity, however, the earnings are taxed as ordinary income, not at the lower capital gains rate.

One criticism of annuities is that they convert capital gains into ordinary income, and you lose a tax break. With a variable annuity, you hope your investments produce huge capital gains. Unfortunately, when you take money from a variable annuity, it's taxed as ordinary income, and you don't get the much lower tax rates on capital gains.

With smart investment decisions and a cooperative stock market, you can achieve a greater rate of return than you'll get with a fixed-income annuity. That was not the case for the woman from Boca Raton who wrote the letter to *The Wall Street Journal*. She was much more comfortable with a guaranteed source of income that did not fluctuate with the stock market. Variable annuities do not seem nearly as appealing during a bear market.

New annuity products will continue to be developed. One relatively new product combines the steady stream of income payments from a fixed-rate immediate annuity with a variable annuity that has a number of investment options. You can create your own version of this product by buying two separate annuities, a fixed and a variable. You can guarantee a specific return with part of your money and seek growth with the variable annuity. By buying separate annuities, you'll give yourself more flexibility.

## EQUITY INDEXED ANNUITIES

In recent years, equity indexed annuities were introduced. The equity indexed annuity is a variation of the fixed annuity. The interest rate is tied to a stock index such as the S&P 500. When the market is down, the equity indexed annuity guarantees a minimum interest rate. Like a fixed annuity, the equity indexed annuity isn't viewed as a security subject to SEC regulations.

If you're considering an equity indexed annuity, make sure you know which index the insurance company is using. Some companies are tying their annuity products to the Dow, Nasdaq, Russell, and other indexes, but the S&P 500 is the most common.

Make certain you understand how your interest credit is calculated. The insurance company may use an averaging method to calculate the credit. There will be a cap on the interest that is added to your equity indexed annuity. The equity indexed annuity isn't designed to beat investing in the stock market, but it can outpace inflation.

Equity indexed annuities are very complicated investment products. It's difficult to compare one company's equity indexed annuity with another's. Make sure you understand how fees and expenses are calculated, because the formula will be quite complicated. There is usually a cap on the upside potential of the equity indexed annuity.

## BEFORE YOU BUY AN ANNUITY TO PROTECT YOUR RETIREMENT

Deciding whether to buy an annuity is a big decision. Once you've invested your money, it's difficult to change your mind without paying a penalty. The surrender charge typically applies if you cash out before a designated date.

The surrender charge is the insurance company's way of recapturing the commission it paid to the salesperson. It should be spelled out in the annuity contract. Surrender charges vary from company to company.

You can find annuities with little or no surrender fees and low expense ratios. These products are referred to as no-load annuities. You pay less, because you're investing directly with the insurance company or financial services provider instead of buying from an agent.

The annuity contract should allow for partial withdrawals. Typically, you can take out 10 percent of the accumulated cash value in a year. This provision in the contract will be useful if you need to tap the annuity for funds during the years the surrender charge is in effect. In addition to the penalties imposed by the contract, taking money from an annuity may result in tax penalties as well. You might owe a 10 percent premature distribution charge to the IRS if you're younger than 59 1/2.

Even if you're not subject to surrender charges, be wary when making an exchange of one annuity for another. The annuity salesperson may not have your best interests at heart and is "churning." Essentially, the salesperson is pushing you to turn in one perfectly good annuity for another to get the sales commission. If the new annuity turns out to be less than you bargained for, you'll have a new surrender charge to worry about for the next five to ten years.

You can exchange one annuity for another without causing yourself tax problems. Section 1035 of the Internal Revenue Code allows for the tax-free exchange of one annuity contract for another. For example, if you're unhappy with the rate of return on your fixed annuity, you may want to exchange it for a variable annuity. You might also want to exchange one company's annuity for another's if you're worried about the financial health of the insurance company from which you purchased the annuity. You won't have a tax problem because of the exchange, but you still have the surrender charge to consider.

## EVALUATING THE COMPANY SELLING THE ANNUITY

The appeal of annuities is that you can choose a payout option that will guarantee an income for life. To assure that lifetime income, however, the insurance company backing the annuity must be around longer than you are.

You want the insurance company to be around to make those payments during what you hope will be a lengthy retirement. Therefore, before buying an annuity, you need to evaluate the financial strength of the company that's selling it. Even if you're not a Certified Public Accountant, you're in luck. There are independent rating services that analyze the financial health of insurance companies.

### A.M. Best rating

A.M. Best is a respected independent rating organization. It provides a well-researched opinion of an insurance company's ability to meet its obligation to policyholders. Although the A.M. Best rating is very reliable, some companies with high marks have run into financial problems.

A + + and A + means the carrier has a superior rating. A and A- are considered to be excellent ratings. B + + and B + are very good ratings. Grades below B + are classified as Vulnerable Best's Ratings.

When you're shopping for an annuity, focus on companies with an A + + or A + rating. If a company hasn't been around long enough to warrant a high letter grade rating from A.M. Best, it's a riskier investment. To find a company's rating, you can visit the A.M. Best website at www .ambest.com.

## Other rating services

Be sure to get a second or third opinion regarding an insurance company's financial health. Standard & Poor's Insurance Rating Services (www .standardandpoors.com) range from AAA to CC. Fitch Ratings (www .fitchratings.com) offers reports on insurance companies too. Another place to look is Moody's Investors Service, Inc. (www.moodys.com).

Weiss Research, Inc. can also be used to research the financial health of the insurer. Weiss Research, as a general rule, provides the most skeptical report on the insurance company's financial well-being. The rating service can be reached at 800-289-9222 or on the Internet at www .weissinc.com.

In an interview on *The Nightly Business Report* on September 2, 2002, Martin Weiss recommended that an insurance company have a rating of B + or higher. According to Weiss, the D rating from Weiss stands for "dangerous," and investors should avoid those companies with that rating.

## Do your own research

Don't rely upon the insurance salesperson to tell you the ratings of the companies from which you're buying a policy. Often, your state's insurance department can provide the financial ratings of insurance companies from A.M. Best or some other service. You can also stop by a good business library to see if any of these ratings are available.

Watch out for agents who downplay the financial ratings of the insurance company backing the annuity. They'll insist that you're protected by a guaranty fund or insolvency fund in your state. When a state guaranty fund is forced to intervene on behalf of a financially troubled insurance company, you won't necessarily get the same terms or payout on the annuity you purchased. It might be a while until you receive your checks as the fund works out the details. While you're waiting, you might be short on cash and sleep as you worry about your annuity.

Being protected by a guaranty or insolvency fund isn't the same as being covered by the FDIC or FSLIC. Remember, too, that even though you buy an annuity at a bank, it is not insured.

## PAYOUT OPTIONS WITH ANNUITIES

When it's time to retire, most people are ready to begin the payout phase of their annuity. It's time to convert the annuity's accumulated value into a guaranteed stream of income. The term "annuitize" refers to the point in time when you begin to receive payments from an annuity. When it's time to annuitize, you want to collect as much as you can for as long you can.

The straight life payment option generates the most income. To calculate the straight life payout, or any payout for that matter, the insurance company examines the life expectancy tables. The company also looks at its expenses and how much money it can make on your investment. If you live longer than the insurance company expects, it loses money on you, but makes up the difference by selling annuities to thousands of others. You get the short end of the stick, however, if you die soon after payments begin, because your beneficiaries get nothing.

A way to cut the risk associated with the straight life payout is to choose the life payout with term certain. You still get a monthly income for life, no matter how long you live, but your loved ones can still collect if you don't live a specified number of years, usually somewhere from ten to twenty years. If you only receive checks for eight years before dying and the guarantee is ten years, your beneficiary receives payment for the remaining two years. Because of the guaranteed payment that the insurance company owes, the payout is less than with the straight life option.

Another way to reduce the financial risk of dying prematurely is by selecting the cash refund payout. The annuity pays income for life, no matter how old you live to be. If you die before getting all of your premiums back, however, the insurer refunds the remainder to your beneficiary in one lump sum. Unfortunately, your beneficiary doesn't receive the earnings on your original investment. The installment refund payout option is similar to the cash refund payout. Your beneficiary is entitled to what's left of the premium you paid, but it's paid out in installments instead of a lump sum.

The joint-and-survivor annuity pays income for the life of two people. Even if one of them dies, the annuity payments continue. Since the insurance company is much more likely to be making payments for a longer period, the monthly payout is less than if that same man or woman chose the straight life payout. This particular payout option works well for a couple that wants an income for as long as both of them live.

The payout options can be structured to meet your specific needs. The down side is that the income you're getting isn't going to buy as much twenty years from now. One solution is an immediate annuity that contains an inflation feature. Another approach is to make sure you have other investments that will keep pace with inflation.

Generally, once you've chosen a payout option, you can't change it. One reason is that if you choose a straight life payout and then develop a terminal illness, some other payout option is going to look much better. Nevertheless, some annuity companies are trying to put more flexibility into the payout stage and will allow you to access some or all of the remaining principal. Some insurers charge for this liquidity feature.

Once you begin receiving payments from your annuity, you'll pay taxes on a portion of it. Part of your payment will be principal, which is not taxable, and the rest will be subject to income tax. The company making payments on your annuity can tell you what portion of your payment is taxable.

## ANNUITY TIPS FROM LINDA LUBITZ, CFP, MIAMI, FLORIDA

Named one of the top 250 financial advisers by *Worth* magazine for eight years straight, Linda Lubitz offers these annuity tips.

> When you annuitize, select a minimum of a ten-year payout, so heirs are protected if you die very prematurely.

> Determine how much income you need over and above your Social Security benefits and pension. Purchase an immediate annuity to guarantee that amount of cash flow. If the market drops again in the future, your income needs are still met.

> Invest the rest of your money for growth. These investments will supplement your guaranteed cash flow. You'll still have enough to live on, even if there's a downturn in the market.

## WEBSITES FOR COMPARING ANNUITIES**

www.annuityscout.com

www.annuityshopper.com

www.annuity.com

**(These sites may not display all of the lowest-cost annuities like Vanguard or TIAA-CREF.)

# PROTECTION TIPS

Annuities are worth including in your blueprint for protecting and re-building your retirement. You can lock in an income for life with an immediate fixed annuity, and that's particularly comforting if you don't have a pension or the stock market scares you. The annuity can provide a safe source of income each month to help pay for your basic living ex-penses. You can use other investments for growth.

When you're investing in fixed annuities, watch out for teaser rates that only last six months to a year. Furthermore, the advertised rate on a fixed annuity may include a first-year bonus. The bonus is paid at the insurance company's discretion and may be withdrawn at any time. Worse yet, if interest rates rise, your annuity won't seem as attractive, and you may not be able to switch annuities without paying a surrender fee.

Another downside with annuities is that in exchange for your life-time income, there is usually nothing left for your heirs. And since the payments from the annuity are normally fixed, the amount you receive may look like peanuts because of inflation over the years.

Even if there is an insolvency fund in your state, you want to feel comfortable that your insurance company will outlive you. It's worth giv-ing up a small amount of monthly income for the peace of mind that comes with buying an annuity from a financially strong insurance com-pany. You might want to split your annuity investment among two or more highly rated companies.

Deferred annuities are an excellent way to put away money for your retirement. Because of the high fees, however, you might want to put as much money as possible in your IRAs and 401(k)s before investing in a deferred annuity. If you do invest in an annuity, look for a no-load, low-cost product.

As products get more complicated and new features are tacked on, it will become more difficult to shop around for the best annuity. You're often left comparing apples and oranges. Decide what features you really need and don't let your decision be influenced by the bells and whistles that one particular annuity offers.

# CHAPTER 7

# Protecting your retirement with real estate investments

AFTER MIAMI DOLPHINS COACH JIMMY JOHNSON GREW WEARY OF COACH-
ing, he retired to the Florida Keys. In a secluded spot by the water, Johnson and his wife live on an estate with twin mansions. The swimming
pool, designed by Johnson, resembles a natural lagoon. The enormous
living room with vaulted ceilings and huge windows offers a magnificent
view of the sea. His boats, a 53-footer and a 30-footer, wait nearby in case
Johnson wants to go fishing or scuba diving.

If you're like most people, your plans for retirement revolve around
real estate, although your dream home may be a bit more modest than
Johnson's. Perhaps, your vision of retirement involves spending more time
in the home you love or buying a new house in an area you've always
dreamed about. It might be near the beach, on a golf course, or in the
mountains. Your dream home might even be in a foreign country.

Real estate investments can be extremely useful in protecting your retirement. In addition to your primary dwelling, assuming you own it, you might opt for other real estate investments such as a second home or a vacation property. Real Estate Investment Trusts (REITs) are also a viable alternative for anyone interested in protecting their retirement. If you're short on money in retirement, reverse mortgages let you stay in your home but use it to generate income.

Real estate can be an albatross or a wonderful investment vehicle. You need to plan carefully to maximize the benefits of real estate investments.

## HOW YOUR HOME CAN PROTECT OR UNDERMINE YOUR RETIREMENT

If you've lived in the same home for the past twenty years, you're in for a surprise. Some prospective buyers are going to walk through your house and react as if they're visiting their grandmother's home. To them, the kitchen you love may look like the one in Barbie's dream house, only smaller. Your bathrooms may look like Lilliputian compared to those being shown in new homes. According to one home-builders group, the average size of new homes has increased in the last fifty years, from 983 square feet in 1950 to 2,225 square feet in 1999.

Before you begin counting how much you'll make on the sale of your home, make sure you're in touch with what buyers want. A four-bedroom, two-and-a-half-bath house may not have the same appeal it once did. Buyers may be looking for a separate bath for each bedroom. They may want a room for a home entertainment system, computers, and other electronic equipment.

In Florida, the market goes in cycles. For a while, two-bedroom homes were quite marketable, because older buyers were scaling down. At some point, however, the market shifted, and older home buyers decided they needed more space and opted for larger houses on one floor, so they wouldn't need to climb steps. Two-story homes are a tough sell in some Florida communities because of the aging population.

The housing market can shift in the blink of an eye. On December 17, 2002, the *South Florida Sun-Sentinel* reported that the frenetic housing market slowed down for homes costing more than $500,000. Reporter Robin Benedict found that houses priced at more than $1 million were not selling at all. A year earlier, these homes were selling quickly.

For most people, their homes have been the most stable investment in their portfolios. Over the years, home prices have risen about 1 percent more than the inflation rate. Home ownership, along with cash, stocks, and bonds, are a big part of most families' wealth. During the recent bear market, many people took comfort from the fact that their homes were increasing in value. Even as their other investments declined in value, their houses gained ground.

## TRADING DOWN

A common retirement planning strategy is to move out of the big house where you raised your children and buy a home that is smaller and cheaper. In theory, this frees up more money for investing and lowers expenses. Most people won't owe any federal income taxes on the sale of their primary dwelling, because the government allows up to $500,000 in profit for married couples and $250,000 for singles. Furthermore, it's no longer a once-in-a-lifetime tax break, as long as the house has been the taxpayer's primary dwelling for at least two years.

Despite the tax break, the trading down strategy doesn't always work. A couple from Westchester County decided it was time to hang it up in July 2002. They chose to build a home in Bonita Springs, Florida. After signing the paperwork and putting money down, the couple put their home in New York up for sale for several hundred thousand dollars more than the home they were buying in Florida.

Before their house went up for sale, it was a seller's market in their area. Buyers were paying more than the asking price for homes. Unfortunately, the home market in the couple's area slowed to a standstill. They lowered their asking price by $100,000, but the reduction still did not result in a buyer. At the same time, their investment portfolio was down significantly. The couple spent many sleepless nights as they adjusted to moving, selling their house, and retirement.

The couple eventually sold their house, but the check they received at the closing barely paid for the one they were building. If the sale fell through, they would have been forced to liquidate investments and withdraw heavily from their retirement accounts. Furthermore, the collapse of the stock market in 2000 through 2002 had depleted their assets significantly.

## MISTAKES YOU CAN'T AFFORD TO MAKE

Real estate can anchor your portfolio in a bear market, but there are many serious mistakes you can make. A woman sold her home in Stuart, Florida, and invested the money in the stock market. She thought her money would grow faster in the stock market than in real estate. When we last checked, the woman had lost all of the money she made on the sale of her home. She wound up being sorry she sold her house.

There is a psychological component with any investment, and selling your home is no different. When you first put your home on the market, you probably have great expectations. Those expectations may have been inflated by a realtor who overstated the value of your house in order to get the listing. Because of those expectations, most sellers will initially be wedded to their selling price and might turn down even a fair offer. As the months go by and buyers are scarce, the seller might welcome any offer. As sellers get more desperate, they are willing to accept an offer they would have been insulted by in the first few weeks the property was on the market.

If and when sellers get an offer, they might be angry if circumstances force them to accept it. The sellers might feel they are "giving" the house away and will be resentful. Many sellers bank on a particular amount of profit and may make financial commitments on that basis. They bank on the income that never comes. If they've bought a new home, they may find themselves overextended. Even if they're happy with the selling price, blowing the profit in the stock market might leave them angry.

There are lessons to be learned from these situations. Wherever possible, you should wait to make sure your primary dwelling sells before committing to another piece of real estate. If you do go forward on your new home, it might be smart to insist on a contingency clause in case your old home doesn't sell within a particular time frame and above a particular price. If you do sell before buying or building a new home, make sure your money is in a safe place, not in the stock market.

If you want to go forward before selling your old house, make sure you can temporarily juggle the cost of both homes. Buy less of a home than you can afford. To play it safe, rent in the city where you want to move and give yourself time to try out the area before buying a house.

Make sure you're aware of all of the extra costs that come with moving. An interstate move can be very expensive. Your insurance costs may be much higher. For example, a homeowners insurance policy in Florida may be much higher because of the risk of hurricanes. Furthermore, the company you're insured with now may not even write coverage in the state because of the risks.

Even though you're not setting up housekeeping for the first time, many people want all new furnishings and wall coverings for their new house. They might actually believe the decorator who tells them to budget 50 percent of the cost of the home for furniture. Hold off on major purchases until you're settled, both financially and psychologically. Although you want to show off your new home as soon as possible, you don't need to buy every piece of furniture and every accent piece right away.

You're usually better off, especially in a bear market, if you can delay tapping into your retirement savings accounts. Wherever possible, try to tap tax-sheltered accounts last. Hopefully, you won't need to liquidate your investments when prices are down. You might be able to arrange a low-interest margin loan through your brokerage firm. Don't borrow the maximum amount allowed, because the brokerage firm will want to sell some of your securities if the value of your holdings drops.

Another possibility is a home equity loan on the house that isn't selling. Make sure that there are no prepayment penalties and that closing costs are minimal. The loan will be paid off when your house sells. You might also consider a swing loan, so you can close on the new house before selling the old one.

# Making the Most of Your Home in Tough Times

Keeping some of your assets liquid during difficult economic times is extremely important. But if you have cash you wish to invest, where should you put it when the stock market is in turmoil?

When the stock market was booming, many financial planners advised against paying off your mortgage. They advised that if you had a low-interest mortgage, your rate of return would be far greater in the stock market. By paying off the mortgage, you also would lose a great tax deduction. In retrospect, this advice doesn't look too good, especially if you could have paid off your mortgage with the money you lost in the stock market.

In good times or bad, there are compelling reasons to pay off your mortgage if you have the cash. If you can't afford to do that or you're afraid of running short on cash, it still might make sense to gradually prepay your mortgage. Making extra payments is a great way to cut the duration of your loan. The peace of mind you'll get from chipping away at your mortgage or paying it off completely is enormous, even if you might have gotten a better return from some other investment.

Home improvements are another way to put your money to good use during rocky economic times. You may recoup some or all of your costs when you sell the house, and you'll get to enjoy the improvements. According to Remodeling Online's 2000–2001 survey, you'll recoup 88 percent of the cost of a minor kitchen remodeling project. You'll get back 81 percent of what you spend on a bathroom remodeling project.

There are no guarantees that you'll get back any or all of the money you've put into your property. Much depends on the nature of the renovation, the type of neighborhood you live in, and when you plan to sell. The value of some home improvement projects diminishes with time. For example, with each year that goes by, your remodeled bathroom or kitchen looks older and more dated. Generally, adding square footage or creating new rooms adds to the value of the house. On the other hand, adding a swimming pool may be a negative for some potential buyers who have young children.

**APPRAISERS**

A real estate agent isn't necessarily the best person to appraise your house. Here are some other options.

National Association of Master Appraisers (800-229-6262)

www.masterappraisers.org

National Association of Independent Fee Appraisers (314-781-6688)

www.naifa.com

**DO HOME IMPROVEMENTS INCREASE YOUR SELLING PRICE?**

According to an annual survey by *Remodeling Magazine,* you might recover 70 percent or 80 percent of the cost of remodeling a bathroom, adding an attic bedroom, or building a deck. This percentage presumes you'll sell your house about a year after the remodeling job. From that point on, the improvements diminish in value, because they start to show wear.

## REVERSE MORTGAGES

Your retirement dream may be to stay right where you are now. Not everyone wants to move to a warmer climate or scale down to a smaller house. Even though your children have moved out and the house may be a little too big, you want to live out your days in the home that holds so many memories. More than likely, it's in a neighborhood where you feel safe and secure, as well as close to friends and relatives.

The problem is that you may not have the financial means to continue living in the house. The taxes may be high, and the upkeep on an old, big house is expensive. Your utility bills might be significant as well. Although your financial situation would improve immensely if you sold the house, you don't want to consider that option.

The reverse mortgage can help you solve this predicament. Unlike the typical mortgage loan, the reverse mortgage allows you to draw money from your home without selling it. You don't owe payments on the loan, provided you continue to live in the house. In a nutshell, you're converting the equity in your home to a monthly income.

Instead of paying a specified amount per month as you do with a mortgage or home equity loan, you use the reverse mortgage to produce additional income for yourself. The loan, as well as all interest and other charges, is paid back when you die, sell the house, or move elsewhere. With a reverse mortgage, the borrower never owes more than the value of the home at the time the loan is repaid.

There are three methods by which the equity in your home can be distributed to you. It can be distributed in a lump sum when you close on the reverse mortgage. Another possibility is a distribution in the form of a line of credit that allows you to draw cash advances until the equity is exhausted. Your third option is to draw cash monthly for as long as you live in the house.

Many people realize that someday they might need to move. The reverse mortgage doesn't have to tie you to your house forever. If you've taken the reverse mortgage in a lump sum, you can use the money to buy an annuity. Like any annuity, you can choose a payout that pays you an income for life. If later on you decide upon a different living arrangement, you'll still be receiving checks from your annuity.

Reverse mortgages aren't all alike. The amount of cash you'll receive, as well as the costs, will differ from lender to lender. As you shop around for the best home equity loan, make sure you look at the Home Equity Conversion Mortgage offered by the U.S. Department of Housing and Urban Development (HUD) and the Fannie Mae Homekeeper program.

Fannie Mae is an agency of the federal government. The money it borrows from investors is used to offer reverse mortgages and other loans.

Not everyone is eligible for a reverse mortgage. You must be at least 62 and own your own home. All home loans against your house must be paid off before you close on the reverse mortgage. You must live in the home for more than half the year, and it must be your principal residence. There are no asset or income requirements, since the lender does not need to worry about your making the monthly payment.

There are many variables that determine how large a reverse mortgage you can get. If you're older, you can get more money, since it's likely the mortgage will be paid back more quickly. You can get a larger reverse mortgage on a more expensive home. The reverse mortgage of a home in a good neighborhood will be larger than on the same house in a less desirable location. Another important factor is interest rates. When rates are down, you receive a bigger reverse mortgage.

Because the interest rate you're being charged affects the size of your reverse mortgage, be sure to shop around among a number of lenders. The interest rate on reverse mortgages tends to be higher than for traditional mortgages. You also need to compare the points and fees on the loan, because they can be quite steep.

The reverse mortgage can enhance your current lifestyle, but it may cut into the estate you leave for your heirs. The income you receive from a reverse mortgage is tax-free and has no impact on your Social Security benefits. Nonetheless, if you need long-term care someday, the income from your reverse mortgage might keep you from qualifying for Medicaid. The income from your reverse mortgage might also affect your entitlement to Supplemental Security Income (SSI).

## REVERSE MORTGAGE RESOURCES ON THE WEB

AARP: www.aarp.org/revmort; 1-800-424-3410

HUD Housing Counseling Clearinghouse: www.hudhcc.org; 1-888-466-3487

National Center for Home Equity Conversion: www.reverse.org;
1-651-222-6775

U.S. Department of Housing and Urban Development (HUD):
www.hud.gov/rmtopten.html; 1-888-466-3487

Consumers Union: www.consumersunion.org

Motley Fool: www.fool.com/homecenter

## HOMES AWAY FROM HOME

It's easy to justify the purchase of a second home. You can argue it's an investment, and that might in fact be the case. A second home can be a great investment or an albatross that you can't unload. You must determine whether the purchase of a second home is likely to undermine your retirement finances or enhance them.

The purchase of a second house or a vacation home often goes hand in hand with retirement planning. Many people purchase a second home or a vacation home with the intent of retiring in it. Second homes give you the opportunity to see if you like a particular location. Even if it is too small to live in on a full-time basis, you can stay there temporarily while you're searching for the perfect retirement housing arrangement.

According to the National Association of Realtors, 359,000 second homes were purchased in 2001. Prices increased by 26.8 percent in 2001. With low interest rates and a stumbling stock market, second homes became a more attractive investment. Second homes can also let you enjoy a different lifestyle and escape your daily routine. You can use the second home for vacations and rent it whenever you can.

### Tax breaks with second homes

A second home can be a great tax shelter. As long as your debt doesn't exceed $1 million, mortgage interest is generally deductible. The points on the mortgage on a second home aren't deductible in the current year and must be spread over the duration of the loan. You can write off property taxes, no matter how many homes you own and how much you pay. However, if your adjusted gross income is too high, your interest and property tax deductions are limited.

When you own a rental property, whether it's a vacation home or a duplex that you rent out, you may be entitled to some attractive tax breaks. When you rent the property for fourteen days or less, you don't need to report any of the income. If you rent the property for more than fourteen days, call your accountant. There are a number of complex rules affecting how much income you must declare on rental property.

If you rent out a vacation home for more than fourteen days per year, the rental income is taxable but you can claim deductions for depreciation, repairs, utilities, and maintenance. Generally, those deductions cannot exceed your income, but you can deduct up to $25,000 more in rental expenses if you restrict your personal use of the property and your income is below a specified ceiling. To deduct rental expenses in excess of rental income, you can't make personal use of the home for more than fourteen days each year or 10 percent of the number of days the home is rented, whichever is greater.

## BEFORE YOU BUY A SECOND HOME

When you buy a vacation home, there are many issues to consider. The perfect vacation home isn't necessarily a place where you'll want to live in retirement. It might be too small or is otherwise inappropriate as a full-time dwelling. If you choose to live in a condo, carriage home, townhouse, or some other dwelling with shared walls, it's not nearly as private as living in a single family home. In most areas, you'll pay more as you get closer to the ocean, lake, golf course, or other desirable views from your window.

Make sure you understand the true cost of buying a second home. You may be using money that might be invested elsewhere at a higher rate of return. If you're buying in a planned community, there may be costs that you aren't used to paying, such as maintenance fees and special assessments for major expenditures by the homeowners board of directors.

Planned communities often have restrictions on how you can use your property. There may be limitations on renting your house. Short-term rentals may be prohibited. Normally, you'll need approval from the community for decisions you take for granted, like changing the color of your house or installing a particular kind of mailbox.

Finally, remember that time shares are not real estate investments. They are a way of prepaying for your vacation.

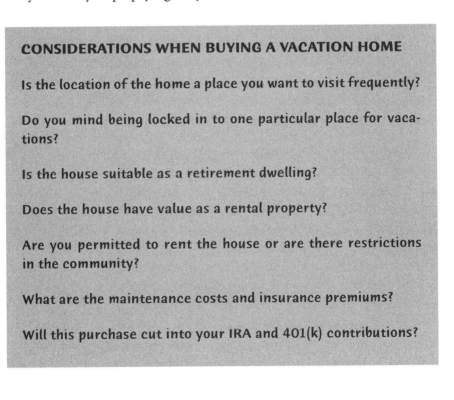

**CONSIDERATIONS WHEN BUYING A VACATION HOME**

Is the location of the home a place you want to visit frequently?

Do you mind being locked in to one particular place for vacations?

Is the house suitable as a retirement dwelling?

Does the house have value as a rental property?

Are you permitted to rent the house or are there restrictions in the community?

What are the maintenance costs and insurance premiums?

Will this purchase cut into your IRA and 401(k) contributions?

## REAL ESTATE INVESTMENT TRUSTS (REITs)

Basically, there are two ways to invest in real estate. You can buy it directly from the owner or you can buy it indirectly through a real estate investment trust, otherwise known as a REIT.

The concept of Real Estate Investment Trusts (REITs) goes back to the late 1800s. REITs are publicly traded companies that own and manage real estate that produces income. This might be an office building, warehouse, shopping mall, apartment complex, hotel, or some other real estate investment. The real estate in the trust is professionally managed.

The tenants that occupy the real estate pay rent. These rents tend to rise during inflationary periods. If space goes unoccupied, however, the rents may barely cover the cost of owning and managing those properties. As an example, when jobs are being slashed, demand for office space will probably decline.

Although REITs invest in real estate, they trade like stock on the major exchanges. They are quite liquid and much easier to sell than real estate that you own directly. The typical REIT has little or no minimum initial investment.

REITs do not pay corporate income tax, which leaves more income to be paid out to investors. To qualify as a REIT, at least 90 percent of the trust's income must be passed on to shareholders in the form of dividends. You'll pay taxes in the current year on those dividends, unless your REIT is held in a qualified retirement plan.

The total return on investing in REITs may be greater than the dividends. The properties within the trust have the potential for capital appreciation.

REITs are a nice addition to a diversified portfolio. They are a good source of current income and a conservative investment. You can use them to offset some of the volatility of your other equity investments.

Some REITs perform better than others, so you need to choose carefully. Look for a solid track record of ten years or more. Find out how the REIT performed during bad economic times. Sniff out a REIT run by seasoned professionals with a history of success.

You also need to investigate the types of real estate the REIT buys. For instance, a REIT may specialize in buying and managing supermarkets and shopping centers rather than office buildings. Another might specialize in industrial properties. The REIT may also limit its purchases to certain geographic areas.

The real estate in a REIT is financed with borrowed money. Therefore, REIT prices tend to fall when interest rates rise. Even the threat of higher interest rates might cause REITs to go down.

Check out the Morgan Stanley REIT index, which measures their performance. You'll also learn more by going to the website of the National Association of Real Estate Investment Trusts (www.nareit.com).

There are mutual funds that invest exclusively in REITs. Shares in these mutual funds tend to move in the opposite direction of stocks. They are often a good way to hedge risk in a bear market.

Don't confuse REITs with REOCs, which are Real Estate Operating Companies. REOCs aren't required to distribute 90 percent of all income. REOCs may reinvest that income, rather than distributing it, in an attempt to achieve more growth.

## PROTECTION TIPS

The blueprint for protecting and rebuilding your retirement is built around where you want to live and how you want to spend your time. Your home and your other real estate investments can enhance your lifestyle in retirement. They can also shelter you from the next financial storm that may hit tomorrow or years from now.

Real estate investments can protect your retirement, but they might also undermine your financial situation and create cash flow problems. Retirement is one of the worst times to be house poor. Financial problems can result from being overextended, and that's particularly dangerous if you're retired and your income is getting smaller, not bigger.

Don't spend the profits from the sale of your home until the buyer shows up with a check at the closing. Remember that a closing isn't a closing until the closing, and a lot can go wrong until that time.

A seller's market can turn into a buyer's market in the blink of an eye. You can't bank on home profits continuing to rise. The real estate market is cyclical. There can be a slump in home sales in your area, even if housing prices are rising nationally. Remember too that you still need a roof over your head, and the cost of your dream house may rise the same or more than the house you're selling.

Rome wasn't built in a day, and your new retirement home in Naples, Florida, doesn't have to be furnished in a week. Take your time when decorating that new house. You'll avoid mistakes made in haste, and you can wait for sales on the furniture and wall coverings. By taking your time, you'll have more control over your spending.

You may be able to afford an expensive house or a second home, but make sure the cost doesn't adversely impact your retirement savings program. It might force you to contribute less to your retirement accounts. You might forgo contributions to a 401(k) retirement savings plan and will miss out on your employer's contribution, as well as tax-sheltered growth in the account.

Real estate is an important part of a diversified portfolio. A small percentage of your retirement portfolio should be in REITs.

When you're ready to retire, keep traumatic lifestyle changes to a minimum. For most people, retiring and moving are huge steps that shouldn't necessarily occur simultaneously.

# CHAPTER 8

# Protecting your Individual Retirement Accounts

IN AN EDITORIAL CARTOON, AN OLDER MAN IS COMBING THE BEACH WITH a metal detector. Another man strolling by asks him, "How's your retirement plan?" The older man replies, "This is it."

Hopefully, the sorry state of your retirement plan won't force you to scour the beach for coins and valuables. Your Individual Retirement Account (IRA) should make you feel better about the future, not worse. Anyone who's serious about saving and investing for retirement is contributing $250 per month or more to an IRA. Nevertheless, you're probably not in the mood to extol the virtues of the IRA if your statements show you have less money in your account than you contributed over the years.

Worse yet, you may already be retired and are watching the value of your IRA plummet. The IRA that was supposed to help you live large during your retirement is not nearly as large as it was supposed to be.

Suppose you had $500,000 in an IRA before the bear market and you're now down to $300,000. If you plan to withdraw 4 percent of your IRA each year, you've gone from $20,000 per year to $12,000, and that can make a big difference in your lifestyle.

Whether you're young or old, a bear market can suck the life out of your IRA. Suppose you opened an IRA five years ago and have contributed $2,000 per year. Instead of having $10,000 plus five years' worth of earnings, you might have much less than $10,000.

Your IRA can still protect your retirement if you fully fund it and take advantage of catch-up contributions. You also need to invest your IRA wisely to rebuild it and protect it from further damage.

## BACK TO BASICS

Traditional IRAs offer an immediate deduction, along with a tax-deferred retirement account. The IRA shelters your money, even after you retire. The earnings continue to compound and escape taxation until you're ready to withdraw funds from them. Assuming you wait until age 59½ or older to withdraw money or meet other conditions, you won't owe the 10 percent penalty on premature withdrawals from an IRA.

Roth IRAs are named after former Senator William Roth from Delaware, who was instrumental in passing the legislation that authorized them beginning in 1998. Although you can't deduct contributions to a Roth IRA, all of your money and earnings is sheltered from taxes. The best feature is that qualified distributions are tax-free, as long as you leave the money in the account for at least five years and you're 59½.

Just as with the traditional IRA, there are circumstances that allow you to withdraw funds from the Roth IRA before the magic age of 59½. In most of those circumstances, you'll avoid the 10 percent premature distribution penalty. More importantly, you'll avoid both the penalty and federal tax on Roth IRA withdrawals if distributions are made because of your disability or death, or for first-time homebuyer expenses.

The maximum annual contribution to traditional IRAs and Roth IRAs was increased to $3,000 in 2003. Assuming the tax laws don't change again, the annual IRA contribution limit will increase gradually until it reaches $5,000 in 2008. After 2008, the limits will rise with inflation. These increases are only authorized until 2010.

## IRA CONTRIBUTION LIMITS (TRADITIONAL AND ROTH)

|            | UNDER 50 | OVER 50 |
|------------|----------|---------|
| Tax Year   | Cap      | Cap     |
| 2003-2004  | $3,000   | $3,500  |
| 2005       | $4,000   | $4,500  |
| 2006-2007  | $4,000   | $5,000  |
| 2008       | $5,000   | $6,000  |
| 2009-2010  | Indexed to inflation | |

## Catch-up contributions

There is also a catch-up provision that lets you contribute an additional $500 per year if you're over 50. To take advantage of the catch-up provision, you must attain age 50 before the end of the taxable year. In 2003, if you're over 50, you can contribute $3,500 to an IRA. Beginning in 2006, you can contribute $1,000 more than the cap if you're over 50.

## CATCH-UP CONTRIBUTIONS

| TAX YEAR  | CAP    |
|-----------|--------|
| 2002-2004 | $500   |
| 2006-2010 | $1,000 |

## Saver's credit

There's also a saver's credit that gives you an additional tax incentive to contribute to an IRA or 401(k). The saver's credit, authorized by the 2001 tax law, gives a tax credit of up to 50 percent of amounts contributed to an IRA or 401(k). A tax credit does much more for the taxpayer than a tax deduction. The credit, as it currently stands, will be available from 2002 until 2006.

The saver's credit is an incentive for lower-income workers to contribute to an IRA or a 401(k). The saver's credit gives an additional income tax break to taxpayers who are 18 or older and meet certain criteria. They can't be full-time students and cannot be claimed as dependents on someone else's return. If they're married and filing jointly, their adjusted gross income must not exceed $50,000. If they're in the single filing status, their adjusted gross income can't exceed $25,000.

The largest tax credit goes to those with the lowest income. For example, a married couple with an adjusted gross income of $30,000 or less receives a 50 percent credit for contributions to qualified retirement plans. The same married couple might only get a 20 percent or a 10 percent credit if their income is higher. The credit is a percentage of your qualified contribution.

# COMPARING THE ROTH IRA AND THE TRADITIONAL IRA

Gilda Radner's character on *Saturday Night Live*, Emily Litella, used to go on a tirade about a particular subject, only to find out that her basic assumption was flawed. Upon finding out that she was way off base, Emily would say, "Well, never mind."

Before launching into a comparison of the Roth IRA and the traditional IRA, it is important to note that many high-income wage earners won't qualify for the traditional IRA, and the forthcoming discussion is moot. Many extremely high-income wage earners won't qualify for either the traditional IRA or the Roth IRA. Let's discuss those earnings limits first, so we don't have to end this discussion with, "Well, never mind."

You won't be eligible for a traditional IRA in 2003 unless your adjusted gross income is below $70,000, if married, and $50,000, if single. And you might not be able to make a full contribution if you're near that ceiling. On the other hand, spouses who don't work may be eligible to participate, even if their husbands or wives are not allowed to make a contribution to a traditional IRA. You don't have to worry about the income eligibility limits for traditional IRAs if neither spouse is covered by an employer-sponsored retirement plan such as a 401(k).

### TRADITIONAL IRA INCOME LIMITS

| TAX YEAR | SINGLE FILERS | JOINT FILERS |
|---|---|---|
| 2003 | $40,000–$50,000 | $60,000–$ 70,000 |
| 2004 | $45,000–$55,000 | $65,000–$ 75,000 |
| 2005 | $50,000–$60,000 | $70,000–$ 80,000 |
| 2006 | $50,000–$60,000 | $75,000–$ 85,000 |
| 2007 | $50,000–$60,000 | $80,000–$100,000 |

Roth IRAs have much higher income eligibility limits, and more people qualify to open an account. You may qualify to make a full or partial contribution if your modified adjusted gross income is between $95,000 and $110,00, if single. If you're married, you may qualify to make a full or partial contribution if your modified adjusted gross income is between $150,000 and $160,000.

The traditional IRA is a tax-deferred investment account. Qualified withdrawals from a Roth IRA are tax-free. Although you lose the immediate tax deduction with a Roth IRA, every penny it makes is going to be yours someday without the IRS taking a chunk.

The contribution to a traditional IRA gives you an immediate tax break, which lowers your adjusted gross income. But when the money comes out, it is taxed as ordinary income, even if it comes from the sale of stock or mutual funds. The tax rates on ordinary income are higher than for capital gains from the sale of stock and mutual funds. You also may get thrown into a higher tax bracket, because of the withdrawals from a traditional IRA.

There are no mandatory withdrawal requirements with Roth IRAs. You don't need to begin withdrawing money at age 70½. You can allow the money to continue growing tax-free.

## IRA Transfers and Rollovers

The bank, mutual fund, or brokerage firm that manages your IRA is called a trustee or custodian. You can transfer your IRA from one trustee or custodian to another without causing yourself a tax problem. These direct transfers are not subject to any taxes or penalties. The IRS places no limits on the number of times you can transfer an IRA each year.

Although the IRS doesn't mind you transferring an IRA from one trustee to another, the trustee may try to discourage you. There may be a fee to close your account or some other penalty imposed. Always check the paperwork you received when the IRA was opened. In addition, the transfer may take longer than you think it should.

Often, individuals take a distribution or payout from their IRA, instead of having the funds transferred directly to another IRA trustee or custodian. By doing so, they risk paying taxes and penalties for a premature withdrawal. To avoid those taxes and penalties, the distribution or payout must be rolled over to another IRA in sixty days or less. Unlike direct transfers, you are only permitted one rollover in a twelve-month period.

As we'll discuss in Chapter 14, you can't transfer your money from a traditional IRA to a Roth IRA without paying taxes on the amount converted. Nevertheless, this may be a smart long-term decision, especially if the value of your traditional IRA assets are considerably lower than they once were.

If you have a 401(k) or some other type of employer-sponsored retirement account, you may be able to roll over the proceeds into an IRA.

You can't roll it over into a Roth IRA, because then the money will escape taxes. If you want it to end up in a Roth IRA, you would need to roll it over first into a traditional IRA and then convert that account to a Roth IRA.

Even though you have sixty days to roll over your IRA to another trustee or custodian, some people take the distribution and use the funds for sixty days. There are no taxes or penalties owed, as long as every cent is rolled over in sixty days. If the money is not rolled over in sixty days, it will be viewed as a premature distribution and subject to penalties, as well as taxes. Rollovers aren't meant to be a short-term loan.

### A TIP FROM MARTIN NISSENBAUM, DIRECTOR OF RETIREMENT PLANNING, ERNST & YOUNG

If your IRA distribution comes directly to you, the trustee is required to withhold 20 percent for the IRS. Therefore, if your IRA is worth $20,000, you'll receive only $16,000, and the trustee will hold on to $4,000 for taxes. Since you must roll over the full $20,000 in sixty days, you'll need to come up with an additional $4,000 of your own money. This situation might dissuade you from rolling over the distribution within the required time frame.

## MANDATORY WITHDRAWALS FROM IRAs

Some people reach their seventh decade and still don't need to tap tax-sheltered retirement accounts. The IRS, however, is ready to take its share of the money.

As mentioned above, if you have a Roth IRA, no mandatory withdrawals are required. With a traditional IRA or retirement accounts like a 401(k), a minimum withdrawal is required. You must make your first withdrawal by age 70½ or by April 1 of the following year at the latest.

Nevertheless, if you wait until April 1 of the following year, you still must make your second withdrawal by December 31 of that same year. As a result, you'll have two withdrawals in the same year, which is quite likely to throw you in a higher tax bracket.

You'll be a very unhappy camper if you fail to make mandatory withdrawals beginning at age 70½. The penalties are quite harsh. Failing to make the appropriate mandatory withdrawal can expose you to penalties of 50 percent of the amount that should have been withdrawn.

The IRS has simplified its mandatory withdrawal rules. Smaller distributions are required, because life expectancies have gone up. Under the old rules, it paid to choose an extremely young beneficiary if your goal was to take out as small an amount as possible. Now, the age of your beneficiary usually won't affect the size of your mandatory distribution. If you have a much younger spouse, however, you can base your withdrawal on the joint life and last survivor life expectancy table.

---

**WEBSITES WITH IRA INFORMATION**

Roth IRA Advisor: www.rothira-advisor.com

Roth IRA Incorporated: www.rothirainc.com

Roth IRA: www.rothira.com

Fairmark: www.fairmark.com/rothira

---

## INVESTING YOUR IRA

When investing the funds in your IRA, you have a wide variety of investments to choose from, and that sometimes makes the decision more difficult. As with any investment decision, you must look at your objectives and risk tolerance. You must consider how your IRA affects your overall asset allocation. You should rebalance your IRA periodically along with your other assets.

As mentioned earlier, there is considerable debate over whether the value or growth approach to investing is more successful. Fund managers who focus on value buy stocks that currently trade at a lower figure than what investors believe is their true worth. Usually, these stocks have low price-to-earnings (P/E) ratios. The fund manager looks for stocks with a relatively low price compared to the company's current earnings.

The growth fund manager invests in stocks with the potential to have future earnings growth. As those earnings grow, the price of the stocks should rise. Although these stocks have a bright future, they normally have high price-to-earnings ratios and low dividend payouts.

You should attempt to blend both styles of investing in your IRA. Divide the stock portion of your IRA among mutual funds that utilize both strategies.

## PROTECTION TIPS

IRAs are an integral part of almost every blueprint for protecting and rebuilding your retirement. By taking advantage of higher contribution limits and catch-up contributions, you can repair some of the damage that occurred during the recent bear market.

You should plan for your money to stay in tax-sheltered retirement accounts for as long as possible. IRAs grow faster, because their growth isn't eaten away by taxes. Although there are ways to make penalty-free withdrawals from an IRA before age 59$^1$/$_2$, you're better off leaving money in your retirement accounts for as long as you can. Tapping IRAs early might undermine your retirement savings.

With traditional IRAs, mandatory withdrawals must begin by age 70$^1$/$_2$ or you'll face a stiff penalty. Make sure you understand the new, simplified rules regarding mandatory distributions. The Roth IRA has no mandatory withdrawal requirement.

If you have a choice between a Roth and a traditional IRA, the Roth might be your best bet. Although you're giving up an immediate tax deduction, you will save thousands in taxes on the earnings that will hopefully accrue over the years. Qualified withdrawals from a Roth IRA are tax-free.

# CHAPTER 9

# Protecting your 401(k) and other

# retirement savings plans

A JULY 2002 *WASHINGTON POST* ARTICLE TOLD THE SAD STORY OF A FOR-
mer WorldCom employee who invested all of her retirement contributions
in company stock. She told *The Washington Post* that the value of her
401(k) retirement savings plan fell from $45,000 to $210.

WorldCom's bankruptcy hurt the financial situation of numerous
former employees and led many of them to seek other opportunities.
Three hundred female WorldCom employees submitted photos in response to a request from *Playboy* magazine. A dozen were featured in the
December 2002 issue in a spread called "The Women of WorldCom."

If you're like most people, the bear market pummeled your retirement savings plan. Your 401(k) probably looks like Rocky Balboa's face
after his fight with Apollo Creed. You may need to counterpunch to avoid
further damage. Whether you make $401,000 per year or $401 per week,
these retirement savings plans can make the difference between a secure
future and one that's filled with financial uncertainty.

Employees who participate in 401(k) retirement savings plans tend to be passive investors. These employees contribute money each payday into an investment they may have chosen years ago. To protect your retirement, you need to stay on top of your 401(k) and other retirement savings plans.

## BACK TO BASICS

The 401(k) is a tax-sheltered account that enables you to put away money for retirement. This type of retirement plan takes its name from the Internal Revenue Code provision that describes how the plan works. Unlike the traditional pension, which is a defined benefit plan, the 401(k) is a defined contribution plan. A defined contribution plan specifies what the employee may contribute, rather than what benefit the employee receives after a certain number of years of employment.

### How 401(k)s work

The mechanics of the 401(k), and similar retirement savings plans, are relatively simple. The percentage of your pay that you choose to invest goes into your 401(k) plan before you get your hands on it. These pretax contributions to a 401(k) reduce your current taxable income. The money grows in a tax-sheltered account.

Although there has been talk in Congress of a Roth 401(k) which would allow for tax-free withdrawals, you pay taxes on all of the money withdrawn from a 401(k) and similar retirement savings plans. The withdrawals are taxed as ordinary income, even if most of the earnings are profits from the sale of stock. Typically, however, you're retired when withdrawals are made, and you are in a lower tax bracket.

Most employers match all or part of the employee's contribution up to a specified amount. The employer's contribution won't necessarily be in cash. Some employers match the employee's contribution with company stock. Legislation is being considered that would keep employers from overloading retirement savings plans with company stock. One proposal would allow workers to sell company stock after three years. Enron employees couldn't sell their shares before age 50.

The IRS now allows companies to enroll employees automatically in 401(k) plans. The onus is then on the employee to opt out of the plan. When an employee is automatically enrolled in a 401(k), the company usually puts 3 percent of the worker's salary in a money market or stable-value investment option. Otherwise, employees who are automatically enrolled might accuse the company of taking too many risks with the investment.

## Vesting

Thanks to the Economic Growth and Tax Relief Reconciliation Act of 2001, you don't need to wait as long for your employer's contribution to vest. Previously, if your employer opted for the gradual vesting schedule, all employer contributions had to be fully vested after seven years of employment. Now, if your employer utilizes a gradual vesting schedule, you are entitled to every penny of the company's matching contribution beginning in 2002 if you're employed for at least six years. You must be at least 20 percent vested after two years of employment. Each year thereafter, you must be vested for another 20 percent of your employer's contribution until you're 100 percent vested.

If your employer utilizes an all-or-nothing vesting schedule called cliff vesting, you don't get any of the company's contribution if you leave before three years of employment. If you last three years, however, you're entitled to the employer's full contribution. Before the latest law went into effect, you needed to wait five years at some companies for the employer's contribution to fully vest.

The new vesting rules make it even more important to participate in a 401(k) offered by your employer. Even if you don't expect a long tenure with that company, the employer's contribution may vest sooner than you think. Aside from the employer's contribution, participating in a 401(k) forces you to save and provides valuable tax breaks. Remember, however, that your employer may apply the shorter vesting schedule to 2002 and later matching contributions, and the prior vesting schedule applies to earlier matching contributions.

The accelerated vesting schedule that began in 2002 does not prevent an employer from adopting 401(k) rules that are even more favorable to the employee. To attract good people, some companies implement a 401(k) that permits an employee to join the plan soon after being hired. The employer's contribution on the employee's behalf vests soon thereafter.

## Early withdrawal? Please don't!

After you've left your place of employment, the best way to ensure the growth of your 401(k) is to keep your hands off it. It's a retirement savings plan, not an ATM machine. Unless certain events occur, most of which are bad, you can't touch the money until age 59½ without paying a 10 percent penalty. You can avoid the penalty, but not the taxes, if money is withdrawn in any of the following situations:

- You are age 59½ or older.
- You die.
- You are disabled.
- You are subject to a Qualified Domestic Relations Order (QDRO).
- You're older than 55 and separated from service.
- You're under 59½, and take substantially equal withdrawals based upon your life expectancy.
- You have medical expenses not covered by insurance that exceed 7.5 percent of your income.

To avoid both the 10 percent penalty and taxes, the money should be rolled over into an IRA.

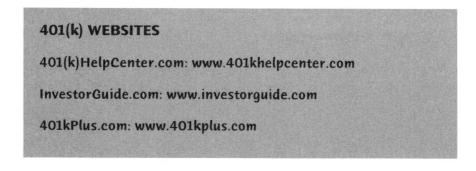

**401(k) WEBSITES**

401(k)HelpCenter.com: www.401khelpcenter.com

InvestorGuide.com: www.investorguide.com

401kPlus.com: www.401kplus.com

# Investment Options in 401(k) Plans

Although you need to keep your hands off your 401(k) when you leave a job, you should take a hands-on approach to your investments. Like any investment, decisions about your 401(k) depend upon your financial objectives and your risk temperament. Younger participants tend to be more aggressive investors. No matter if you're young or old, most people who sustained heavy losses during a bear market will lean toward more conservative investments.

You can't ignore your 401(k) during the course of your employment. You're asking for trouble if you make your investment choices on the first day of your employment and stick with them forever. That approach won't necessarily work anymore.

Companies offer at least three investment choices. Usually, that means a stock fund, a bond fund, and a stable value fund. Better plans offer a wider range of choices including money market funds, bond mutual funds, lifestyle funds, balanced funds, growth-and-income funds, index funds, aggressive growth funds, international funds, and company stock. Before investing, you need to understand all of the risks associated with each investment option.

## Money market funds

If you're extremely conservative or you're sitting on the sidelines while waiting for the market to settle down, the money market fund is a good choice. The fund invests mainly in short-term, high-quality debt instruments, such as treasury bills.

## Stable value funds

The stable value fund invests in guaranteed investment contracts (GICs), which pay a fixed interest rate for a specified period of time. GICs normally pay higher interest than a money market fund. The stable value fund invests in GICs that are guaranteed by a number of insurance companies. Your plan may call it by a different name, such as a fixed income fund.

## Bond funds

For the conservative investor, the 401(k) plan may offer bond funds. As we discussed earlier, bond mutual funds aren't as conservative as some people think. Bond mutual funds often earn more than stable value funds but have a higher degree of risk. The manager of the fund buys different bonds with different interest rates and maturity dates. Each day the portfolio changes as bonds are bought and sold. The bonds held in the fund tend to go up in value as interest rates fall and down in value as interest rates rise.

## Lifestyle funds

Some funds are hybrids, investing in stocks, bonds, and cash assets. These hybrid funds help to keep your assets in balance. For example, many good 401(k) plans offer lifestyle funds as an investment option. Lifestyle funds invest in a combination of stocks, bonds, and cash investments based on your age and risk tolerance. Your plan may refer to them as life cycle or life stage funds. You choose a lifestyle fund based on your estimated date of retirement. Generally, the portfolio of a lifestyle fund shifts from stocks to bonds as your designated retirement age approaches.

## Balanced funds

Balanced funds are also viewed as very conservative investments. With a balanced fund, the fund manager chooses a portfolio that is split between stocks and bonds. The fund manager might also purchase preferred stock to generate income and curb risk.

## Growth-and-income funds

Growth-and-income funds tend to be less risky. A significant percentage of the fund's assets are invested in income-producing securities such as dividend-paying stocks and bonds. The fund manager usually selects stocks that have a potential for price appreciation and current income. Frequently, those are companies that pay a healthy dividend and are less volatile than pure growth stocks that pay out little or none of their earnings. Growth-and-income funds have considerable appeal to the 401(k) investor who wants capital appreciation with some measure of safety.

## Index funds

Index funds contain a shopping basket filled with stocks. The fund holds all or a sample of stocks in a particular market index. For example, the S&P 500 is an index of 500 large company stocks. The Russell 2000 is an index of small company stocks. An index fund filled with large company stocks is generally viewed as less risky than an index fund made up of small company stocks. Index funds usually have low expenses, which reduces the risk somewhat.

## Aggressive growth funds

Aggressive growth funds are considered to be quite risky and more volatile than other stock fund investments. The companies in this fund's portfolio have a considerable upside, as well as downside. The fund manager takes risks with the hope of achieving maximum capital gains in a relatively short period of time.

## Global and international funds

To fully diversify your portfolio, you should invest in foreign stocks. Global funds and international funds own many of the same stocks but are slightly different. The global fund must have at least 25 percent of its holdings in foreign stocks. The international fund must keep virtually all of its money in foreign stocks.

## Company stock

The riskiest of all investments in a 401(k) is company stock. Even if you work for a great company, buying too much of its stock is very risky. Even the best companies stumble, and that might happen as you near retirement age. Investing all of your 401(k) money in your employer's stock is extremely dangerous. You may be forced to take your employer's contribution in company stock, but all other money in your 401(k) should be well-diversified.

On the bright side, 401(k) plans must now give participants thirty-day advance notice of "blackout periods" affecting their right to change investments, take loans, or obtain distributions. The blackout period also affects the employee's right to trade company stock.

## WHY INVESTING ENTIRELY IN COMPANY STOCK IS A BAD IDEA

Even great companies suffer from setbacks. If your 401(k) is loaded with company stock, you'll suffer even more when these setbacks occur.

One stock, even a blue-chip, isn't diversification. You should also stay away from stocks in the same industry. Companies in the same industry are likely to be down in value at the same time, since they are affected by the same market conditions.

Your career and your investments are all riding on one company. If your employer runs into problems, your career and your 401(k) will be in jeopardy.

401(k) investing utilizes the dollar cost averaging strategy. That approach is less likely to be successful if you're only investing in one stock.

## DOLLAR COST AVERAGING

Susan Reimer, a lifestyle correspondent for the *South Florida Sun-Sentinel*, wrote that she was through with dollar cost averaging. "I was the High

Priestess of Dollar Cost Averaging," she wrote on September 13, 2002. "I worshipped at the altar of Dollar Cost Averaging. I believed in Dollar Cost Averaging." After watching her 401(k) and other investments plummet, however, Reimer decided that the dollar cost strategy had let her down.

Although thousands of investors are feeling much like Reimer, they shouldn't give up on dollar cost averaging. The dollar cost averaging strategy helps to ensure the long-term profitability of your 401(k) retirement savings plan. The strategy helps you to invest systematically, rather than trying to time the market. Nevertheless, although the strategy is a systematic way to invest your money, it is no guarantee of success.

With dollar cost averaging, you invest the same amount at regular intervals in whatever stock or mutual fund you've chosen. Unless you change your investment mix frequently, you're utilizing dollar cost averaging in your 401(k) each payday. Your contribution buys more shares when prices are low and fewer shares when the price per share is high.

As an example, let's say you invest $200 per month in a stock that's currently selling for twenty dollars per share. Your $200 investment buys ten shares at that price. If the stock falls to ten dollars per share, your $200 investment pays for twenty shares. If the stock goes up to forty dollars per share, your monthly investment buys five shares.

Investing systematically usually beats trying to outguess the stock market. When you invest a lump sum instead of dollar cost averaging, you're trying to time the market, and you risk putting all of your money into an investment at its highest price. With dollar cost averaging, you invest gradually and are more likely to wind up with a favorable price-per-share. When you're ready, sell your holdings.

Even though you're using the dollar cost averaging strategy, you won't necessarily make money. You can still lose money if you need to sell your shares during a bear market. Normally, however, if you hang on and invest regularly through good times and bad, you'll do well in the long run.

## Diversify for better results

Unfortunately, dollar cost averaging works far better with a diversified mutual fund than it does with individual stocks. If you invested regularly in a single stock like Enron or WorldCom, you were buying lots more shares as the price went down, but that doesn't do you any good if you're putting money in a company that's headed for bankruptcy. Sadly, some employees of those companies lost out because their 401(k) plans were not diversified.

### Rebalance periodically

The dollar cost averaging strategy does not require you to stick with the same investment forever. You should rebalance your 401(k) periodically. If your stock portfolio represents too large a percentage of your 401(k), shift assets to bonds or the stable value fund.

Legislation is pending in Congress that would require employers to offer independent investment advice to employees. Although the former high priestess of dollar cost averaging would disagree, those independent investment advisers are likely to recommend that you hang in there with the dollar cost averaging strategy in good times or bad.

## WHEN IT'S TIME FOR YOU TO GO

If you keep investing through bull and bear markets over a long career, you should accumulate a sizable amount in your 401(k). It's extremely important that you thoroughly consider your options when it's time to retire or leave the company. If you're not 59½, taking a distribution from your 401(k) may subject you to taxes and a 10 percent penalty. Even if you are 59½, taking a distribution can cause you an immediate tax problem and will undermine your retirement savings program.

Many people take the distribution instead of rolling over their 401(k) into an IRA or their new employer's plan. A Putnam Investments study found that 30 percent of 401(k) retirement plan participants took the cash instead of rolling over their accounts. Among participants age 18 to 34, 39 percent opted for the money instead of putting the cash away for their retirement. In 2001, these participants paid $8.3 billion in federal taxes and penalties. If you change jobs frequently and cash in your 401(k) each time, you'll have very little put away for retirement.

## Don't blow small distributions

Younger workers in particular make the mistake of blowing their small 401(k) distribution. They fritter away the money and blow the chance to help secure their future. When you fail to roll over a 401(k) distribution, you pay taxes and quite often a 10 percent penalty. You also miss out on how large that account may grow to be. You lose all of the compounded earnings that accrue in a tax-sheltered account.

## Pay back all loans

Keep in mind that when you're ready to leave a job, you must pay back all loans against your 401(k). Failure to pay those loans back in full may be viewed as a premature distribution. You may owe taxes and a penalty on the amount of the loan.

## Options for your 401(k) upon separation from employment

When you're ready to leave a job or retire, you have three options for your 401(k) retirement savings plan. The first is to take a lump sum distribution. If you're at least 59½, or 55 and separated from service, you can take every penny of your 401(k) without a penalty, but you're usually making a mistake. Unless you roll over the lump-sum distribution into an IRA, you'll pay taxes on the full amount and put yourself in a terrible tax bracket.

A second option is to leave the money in the company plan. Just because you're leaving doesn't mean your 401(k) has to come with you. Many companies are happy to let you keep your 401(k) with them, even though you're no longer an employee. Assuming you're satisfied with the investment options and former employees pay no special fees, you can leave the plan where it is now.

The third option is to roll the money over into an IRA or a new employer's plan. You can now roll over your 401(k) into a new employer's plan, even if that new plan is a 403(b) or a 457 plan. If you roll your 401(k) into an IRA at a brokerage firm, you can choose from hundreds of investment options, not just those offered in your new employer's plan. You can put your current holdings in a self-directed IRA, rather than investing the proceeds in your new employer's investment offerings.

Whichever you choose, your safest bet is to have the 401(k) transferred directly to the trustee of your new plan. If the proceeds of your 401(k) are sent directly to you, it is imperative that the money be rolled over within sixty days or you'll pay a penalty and taxes. Since the money in the 401(k) hasn't been taxed yet, it must be rolled over into a traditional IRA, not a Roth IRA.

## STAYING THE COURSE FOR YOUR 401(K)

The 401(k) puts your savings and investing on automatic pilot. You save and invest every payday without any effort on your part.

Turning down free money is no way to protect your retirement. If your employer matches all or part of your 401(k) contribution, put as much money in as you can spare. You'd lose a percentage of that contribution to taxes anyway.

Invest for the long term with growth investments. Unless you're only a few years away from retirement, you won't be touching your 401(k) for quite a while.

Watch your asset allocation mix. Although your instincts are telling you to stay away from stocks, you need to allocate more money into the market if too small a percentage of your assets are in equities. Conversely, when the market is booming, stocks usually make up too large a percentage of your assets. You might have reduced the damage caused by the recent bear market if you had rebalanced your portfolio and allocated more money to nonstock investments.

If you've lost money in your 401(k), focus on rebuilding it. The maximum annual pretax contribution was increased from $10,500 to $11,000 on January 1, 2002, and to $12,000 on January 1, 2003. It will continue to rise by $1,000 each year until 2006. The maximum contribution in 2006 is $15,000, and from 2007 to 2010, it will rise in relation to inflation. You can also make catch-up contributions if you're over 50. Even if you're nowhere near the cap, increase your contribution.

## LIMITS FOR 401(K) AND CATCH-UP CONTRIBUTIONS

| CALENDAR YEAR | DEFERRAL LIMIT | CATCH-UP LIMIT |
| --- | --- | --- |
| 2003 | $12,000 | $2,000 |
| 2004 | $13,000 | $3,000 |
| 2005 | $14,000 | $4,000 |
| 2006 | $15,000 | $5,000 |

Your plan may allow an additional catch-up contribution if you have fifteen years or more of service. See www.mpower cafe.com for more details.

## OTHER PLANS

Though most workers in the private sector have 401(k) plans, they are not the only type of employer-sponsored plan.

## 403(b) plans

Take that copy of the Internal Revenue Code that you keep on the night-stand and flip to Section 403(b). A 403(b) plan is much like a 401(k), except that it is designed for employees of public educational institutions such as schools and universities, as well as churches, nonprofit hospitals, museums, and charities. Like 401(k)s, they allow employees to allocate some of their salary before taxes into an account that grows on a tax-deferred basis until withdrawal.

## 457 deferred compensation plans

Employees in the public sector have the opportunity to use a Section 457 deferred compensation plan. They are available to most state and local government employees and are used to put away money to provide supplemental retirement income. The numerical reference to 457 comes from the Internal Revenue Code section. You defer compensation on a pretax basis using payroll deduction. Section 457 plans let you defer federal and sometimes state income taxes until your assets are withdrawn. Section 457 plans contain many of the same features found in 401(k) retirement savings plans that are used in the private sector.

Just as with 401(k)s, the contribution limits for 403(b) and 457 plans are also increasing. They will increase to $15,000 by 2006. From 2007 to 2010, the ceiling on contributions will increase with inflation. If you're age 50 or older, you can make catch-up contributions to 401(k), 403(b), and 457 plans.

## SIMPLE IRAs

Like 401(k)s, a SIMPLE (Savings Incentive Match Plan for Employees) IRA is a salary reduction plan, and the employer contributes the salary reductions to the account set up on your behalf. The employer makes a contribution on your behalf. As with other retirement savings accounts, the salary reduction feature cuts your tax bill right now.

SIMPLE IRAs are designed for the self-employed or an employee of a company with one hundred employees or less. Normally, eligible employees must have received compensation in the previous calendar year of $5,000 or more. The employer may not maintain another qualified plan for employees. Like 401(k)s, SIMPLE IRAs reduce the participant's salary, and the money is put away before income taxes are deducted.

With the SIMPLE IRA, earnings grow in a tax-deferred account and are taxed upon withdrawal. The participant must begin withdrawals by age 70½. You can still contribute to a Roth IRA, even if you have a SIMPLE IRA. Generally, the same withdrawal rules that apply to traditional IRAs are also applicable to SIMPLE IRAs, except there's a 25 percent penalty on the amount withdrawn if you're younger than 59½ and have been in the plan for less than two years. Otherwise, you pay the standard 10 percent penalty on the amount withdrawn.

## RETIREMENT PLANS FOR SMALL BUSINESSES

If you own a business, you can set up a simplified employee pension (SEP), even if the only employee is you. Or you might have a solo 401(k) or Keogh plan.

### Simplified employee pensions

A simplified employee pension (SEP) is a retirement plan that permits employers to make deductible contributions on behalf of participating employees. You'll sometimes hear it called a SEP-IRA. Like a 401(k), a SEP is considered to be a defined contribution plan.

You can contribute and deduct up to 20 percent of self-employment income up to a maximum of $40,000. If that's your only source of income, it's usually tough to put away that much money. On the other hand, if you have a side business that isn't your primary source of income, try to put as much money as possible in the SEP.

### The solo 401(k)

You can have a 401(k), even if you run a one-person business. The solo 401(k) offers much larger deductible annual contributions. The cap on contributions is $40,000, or $42,000 in 2003 if you are 50 or older. One-person 401(k)s tend to be less attractive, because they have high setup fees, as well as filing and administrative charges.

### Keogh plans

Keogh plans are designed for small businesses. You can deduct contributions made to a Keogh and bring down your tax bill. At the same time, you're saving for retirement. Like traditional IRAs, your contributions and earnings are sheltered from taxes until you begin making withdrawals.

There are two types of Keogh plans, a money purchase Keogh and a profit-sharing Keogh. With the money purchase Keogh, you must select a percentage of your net income that you will contribute year after year. You can't change the percentage. Although this type of Keogh is very inflexible, it forces you to save for retirement. You have a higher ceiling on contributions with the money purchase Keogh plan.

With a profit-sharing Keogh, you have more flexibility. If you're having a bad year, you don't have to make any contribution. You can vary your contributions from year to year.

## EMPLOYEE STOCK OWNERSHIP PLANS AND STOCK OPTIONS

The employee stock ownership plan, or ESOP, is a type of profit-sharing arrangement. With these plans, the company contributes shares of its stock to your retirement account or permits you to buy them at a discount from the market price. Usually, the plan permits employees to accumulate money through payroll deduction and use the funds to purchase company stock at a discount.

As mentioned earlier, putting too much money in company stock is a disaster waiting to happen. Nevertheless, you don't want to turn down free shares from your employer. If you're overloaded with company stock in your ESOP, make sure you're not purchasing additional shares with your own money. If you're 55 or older, there are likely to be fewer restrictions on selling that company stock, and it's worth considering if you own too many shares.

It remains to be seen if companies will give out stock options as freely as they have in the past. Some companies are changing their accounting practices and are expensing stock options in the year they are granted. Because they will have a direct impact on current income, companies may be reluctant to grant them.

Before the bear market, stock options were viewed as a way for even low-level employees to get rich. They were offered as an incentive to attract and keep key employees. With Internet stocks flying high, stock options made it possible for thousands of employees to get rich. When Internet stocks ran into turbulence, much of that wealth disappeared.

If you are granted stock options, make sure how much time you have to convert your shares. It might not be as long as you think. You may have less time to convert if you leave the company. With stock options, remember, if you snooze, you lose.

Don't allow your greed to get the best of you with stock options. If you wait for the price of your stock to go higher and higher like many people have, you'll lose the opportunity to convert your stock options at a profit. Speak with an accountant to see how converting your stock options affects your tax situation.

## PROTECTION TIPS

Your retirement blueprint requires contributing as much as you can to your 401(k) or some other employer-sponsored retirement account. If you scream every time you open your investment statements, putting more money away may seem like throwing good money after bad. But save and invest the money anyway. Use the higher contribution limits and catch-up provisions in the tax law as an opportunity to protect and rebuild your retirement savings accounts.

If you weren't making the maximum IRA or 401(k) contributions before the law changed, the catch-up provisions may seem meaningless to you. At 50 or older, you might still have large expenses, like tuition bills for your children, that are keeping you from putting more money away. Nevertheless, to protect your retirement, increasing your contributions must become a top priority.

Maxing out your 401(k) contributions should get easier as you near retirement. At that stage of your career, your income should be at its peak. Putting more away in retirement accounts lets you see how well you'll do with less money coming in. You can practice living on less money, which is essentially a dress rehearsal for retirement.

Since putting away more money in a 401(k) lowers your income, contributions have less impact on your take-home pay. You would have lost some of those contributions in taxes anyway.

Even if you don't expect to be at a job for too long, contribute to the company's 401(k). You may find you'll stay for much longer than you think. Contribute something, even if it's only a small percentage of your pay. Whenever possible, contribute the maximum amount that your employer will match.

Diversify, and don't put too much in your employer's stock. Your 401(k) should be in balance, but it also should be balanced with the assets outside your retirement plan. Rebalance your entire portfolio periodically and avoid panic selling.

When you switch jobs, roll over your 401(k), even if it's only a small amount. Because of tax-free compounding, the amount might grow significantly over the years. If you don't roll it over, you'll pay taxes on the money and a penalty on the amount withdrawn. The extra money might even throw you into a higher tax bracket.

Avoid borrowing from the plan. If you lose your job, you must pay the loan back in full. Otherwise, it will be viewed as a premature withdrawal and you'll pay taxes, as well as a 10 percent tax penalty.

Contributing to your 401(k) may be more important than putting money into your child's custodial account, Coverdell Education Savings Account, or Section 529 college savings plan. While financial aid may make up the difference in your child's college costs, no one's going to make up the difference in your retirement savings. Furthermore, contributing to a 401(k) is particularly important when stock prices are down. You might be better off borrowing for your child's education and putting away more for retirement.

# CHAPTER 10

# Protecting your Social
# Security benefits

IN A TONGUE-IN-CHEEK LETTER TO THE EDITOR OF THE *SOUTH FLORIDA Sun-Sentinel*, Harold Epstein of Coconut Creek, Florida, said he didn't know how to spend his overwhelming Social Security increase of $11 per month. He couldn't decide whether to use it to pay his $300-per-year increase in condo maintenance, his $696-per-year increase for supplemental health insurance, or his $124-per-year increase in homeowners' insurance.

When you're working, you look forward to your annual pay raise. When you're receiving Social Security, your annual pay raise comes on the first day of January. In January 2003, Social Security recipients received a 1.4 percent increase in their monthly benefit check, the smallest increase in four years. At the same time, the cost of their Medicare premiums rose by 8.7 percent, a $4.70 increase, to $58.70 per month.

If your employer gave you a 1.4 percent pay raise and increased the cost of health insurance coverage, the odds are good you'd be in your boss's office in minutes with the door closed. Social Security recipients, however, can't negotiate their pay raise, even though they're paying more for prescription drugs and some must choose between buying food and purchasing medication.

When 401(k) and IRA balances were soaring through the roof, Social Security benefits seemed less important in retirement planning. If your IRAs, 401(k), and your other retirement accounts are a fraction of what they used to be, that guaranteed income from Social Security is looking better and better. Because Social Security benefits are adjusted each year for inflation, they'll protect you to some extent against the erosion of your purchasing power. Nevertheless, you must make the most of your Social Security benefit to protect your retirement.

## BACK TO BASICS

If you're in need of a wake-up call regarding the importance of saving on your own for retirement, consider that roughly two-thirds of Americans over age 65 receive more than half their income from Social Security. The average monthly check for a retired worker is a mere $895 as of January 2003. For married couples, the average check is only $1,483 per month, and the top monthly payment is $1,741.

### How Social Security benefits are calculated

According to the American Association of Retired Persons, or AARP (www.aarp.org), if you made minimum-wage earnings all of your life, your Social Security benefit will replace about 59 percent of your preretirement wages. If you made the maximum wage subject to Social Security taxes, your benefit will be roughly 24 percent of your preretirement earnings. Worse yet, if you earned much more than the maximum amount subject to Social Security taxes, your monthly benefit check represents an even smaller percentage of what you used to make. The top wage in 2003 that is subject to Social Security taxes is $87,000.

If you're depending upon Social Security for most of your income in retirement, you need to protect your job. Losing your job near the end of your career can have a dramatic impact on your Social Security benefit. Your check is calculated based on your thirty-five highest-earning years, which are indexed for inflation and added together. Instead of your last years in the workplace being high-earning years, they might potentially be zero.

If you lose your high-paying job as you approach Social Security age, your Earnings and Benefit Estimate Statement won't look as good. It's based on you continuing to work at an estimated salary until your full retirement age. If you're downsized before reaching that age, you can't bank on the same Social Security benefit in that statement. You might need to take a job at a lower rate of pay, which may affect how much you'll get from Social Security.

You should receive your Earnings and Benefit Estimate Statement each year from the Social Security Administration. If you haven't received it, call 800-772-1213 (TTY 800-325-0778) or look on the Web at www .ssa.gov. Another helpful publication you can get from the Social Security Administration is called *Retirement Benefits* (Publication#05-10035).

## How to apply for Social Security benefits

Don't forget that there are three ways to apply for Social Security benefits. You can apply by calling the Social Security Administration or by going online at www.ssa.gov/applyforbenefits. Your third option is to call the toll-free number and set up an appointment at your local Social Security office.

## GETTING THE MOST FROM YOUR SOCIAL SECURITY

Until recently, the age at which you could receive full Social Security benefits was 65. In 2003, the age to qualify for full benefits is 65 years and two months. It will gradually be increased to age 67. Here's how it works.

| YOUR YEAR OF BIRTH | AGE WHEN YOU RECEIVE BENEFITS |
| --- | --- |
| 1937 or before | 65 |
| 1938 | 65 and two months |
| 1939 | 65 and four months |
| 1940 | 65 and six months |
| 1941 | 65 and eight months |
| 1942 | 65 and ten months |
| 1943–1954 | 66 |
| 1955 | 66 and two months |
| 1956 | 66 and four months |
| 1957 | 66 and six months |
| 1958 | 66 and eight months |
| 1959 | 66 and ten months |
| 1960 or later | 67 |

Even though the full retirement age is rising gradually, you can still receive reduced Social Security benefits at age 62. If you begin collecting at age 62 instead of your full retirement age, however, your benefits will be lower. If you begin collecting at age 62 and your full retirement age is 65, you'll only receive about 80 percent of the check you would get by waiting three years. In addition, if you live long enough, collecting early will eventually result in your receiving less benefits during your lifetime.

Your check is reduced for each month you collect benefits prior to your full retirement age. The benefit is reduced by $5/9$ of 1 percent of the full benefit for each month that you retire before your full retirement age up to a maximum of thirty-six months. For any additional months beyond the thirty-six months, the benefit is reduced by $5/12$ of one percent.

If your full retirement age is 66 and you want to collect Social Security at age 62, here's how the benefit would be calculated. The full benefit would be reduced by $5/9$ of 1 percent for three years. Thirty-six months times $5/9$ of 1 percent equals a 20 percent reduction. You also have to reduce the full benefit for another twelve months, so take twelve times $5/12$ of 1 percent, which equals five. Therefore, you would receive 25 percent less each month than if you waited until your full retirement age of 66.

If your full retirement age is 67, you would need to take another twelve-month reduction. Multiply twelve times $5/12$ of one percent, which results in another 5 percent reduction. Your Social Security benefit would be 30 percent less than if you held off on collecting until your full retirement age of 67.

The decision regarding whether to collect early or not requires you to look at a number of factors including the following:

- Taxes—You may be taxed on your Social Security if your income is too high.

- Employment situation—Unless you've reached the full retirement age, your Social Security check will be reduced if you exceed the earnings threshold.

- Life expectancy—If living to a ripe old age doesn't run in your family, you may want to take the money now and enjoy it.

- Need—If you're doing quite nicely without collecting Social Security benefits, you may wish to hold off until you really need the money.

- Other income—Collecting early may reduce your Social Security check for years to come, but it may help you avoid tapping your IRA and other tax-sheltered accounts. The earnings on those accounts may more than make up for what you may ultimately lose in Social Security benefits.

- Feelings of entitlement—After working for a lifetime, many people feel they deserve to be paid back for all those years of contributions. They can't wait to start collecting.

According to AARP, six of ten retirees begin collecting benefits before their full retirement age.

## SHOULD I GO OR SHOULD I STAY?

Here's a piece of advice that sounds inherently contradictory. You can protect your retirement by not retiring. What you're really doing is delaying your retirement to ensure that you have more than enough to live on for decades to come.

One way to increase the amount of your Social Security check is to work longer. There is a bonus if you wait to collect your Social Security benefits called the delayed retirement credit. If you delay taking Social Security beyond your full retirement age, your benefits increase by a specified percentage each year.

It may not pay to delay receiving Social Security checks. That's extra money you could be investing. Assuming you invest sensibly, you'll probably make more money than you would get from the bonus. If you do delay, you'll get more money each month once your benefits begin, but it will be a long time until you catch up with the Social Security recipients who started collecting at their full retirement age.

The following table shows how much extra Social Security you would get by waiting to collect your benefits. If you were born in 1943 or later, for example, you would receive 8 percent more in your Social Security check for each year you hold back on collecting benefits. No credit is given, however, after age 69.

### INCREASES IN SOCIAL SECURITY BENEFITS FOR WORKING LONGER

| YEAR OF BIRTH | YEARLY RATE OF INCREASE |
|---|---|
| 1917–1924 | 3% |
| 1925–1926 | 3.5% |
| 1927–1928 | 4% |
| 1929–1930 | 4.5% |
| 1931–1932 | 5% |
| 1933–1934 | 5.5% |

| 1935–1936 | 6% |
|-----------|------|
| 1937–1938 | 6.5% |
| 1939–1940 | 7% |
| 1941–1942 | 7.5% |
| 1943 or later | 8% |

Source: Social Security Administration.

## AREN'T I THROUGH WORKING YET?

Unfortunately, the stock market is forcing people out of retirement. Whereas many retirees work to keep busy and active, thousands are now working out of necessity, not choice.

Many people are under the mistaken impression that they can work as much as they want without adversely affecting their Social Security benefit. At full retirement age, you may earn as much as you want without affecting your Social Security benefit check. The new law does not use age 65 as the date when you can make as much as you want, because that is no longer the official retirement age.

If you are younger than that full retirement age and you are collecting Social Security, you may not earn more than $11,520 in 2003. You'll lose one dollar in Social Security benefits for each two dollars you earn over that amount. This harsh penalty is designed to discourage people from collecting Social Security early and then continuing to work. There's a special monthly earnings ceiling that applies in the year you retire. Ask Social Security how your earnings in the year you retire will affect your benefit.

Losing a chunk of your Social Security check will make many people question whether it is worth working at all. Although overall you'll still come out ahead, it may not make economic sense to take a part-time job, especially if you're not enjoying the work. If you're working part-time and making more than the cap when you reach age 62, it may be wise to wait to apply for Social Security benefits.

Keep in mind that only wages from a job or self-employment income will reduce your Social Security benefit. The income you receive from IRA and 401(k) withdrawals will not reduce your benefit. Your stock dividends, interest, and annuity payments will also have no bearing on your Social Security check. Only earnings from working, wages, or self-employment count toward the $11,520 ceiling.

Nevertheless, all of this income will affect whether you'll pay taxes on your Social Security check. If your income is too steep, you'll be forced to pay taxes on a portion of your check.

Working at any age affects whether you'll pay taxes on your Social Security benefits. If you're married and filing a joint return, you must make less than $32,000 to avoid tax on your Social Security check. If your combined income (adjusted gross income, plus nontaxable interest, and half of your Social Security benefits) is between $32,000 and $44,000, up to 50 percent of your Social Security benefit will be taxable. If you earn more than $44,000, up to 85 percent of your benefits will be taxable.

The formula gets quite complicated, so you may need an accountant. For example, your income for determining this tax includes tax-exempt interest. In addition, even if it's you who's receiving Social Security benefits, your spouse's income must be included in the calculation.

## "UNRETIRING" AND SOCIAL SECURITY

Suppose that you decide to collect Social Security benefits before the full retirement age and then have second thoughts. There is a possibility of returning the money and "unretiring." Even some Social Security employees don't realize this is possible.

Let's say you retire at age 62 and begin collecting a lower Social Security benefit. Since you haven't reached the full retirement age, you're subject to the earnings limit. After a few months, you see a great job opportunity that pays far more than your Social Security benefit. Or perhaps you're bored after retiring early, or you're financially strapped and need to go back to work.

If you return the benefits you received, you can decide to "unretire" and notify Social Security as such. When you're ready to retire for good, you will receive a higher benefit than you were getting at age 62. You'll be given credit for the extra years of work, and Social Security will need to recalculate the amount you'll receive. You won't be penalized for changing your mind.

## Protection Tips

For too many people, Social Security is their entire blueprint for retirement. If Social Security benefits are your only source of income in retirement, your future won't be too secure. Nonetheless, make sure you get every penny you're entitled to from Social Security. Check your earnings on the benefits statement. It will be much easier to correct those mistakes now.

Remember that the projections on your benefits statement presume you'll keep working and will earn slightly more each year. A period of unemployment, or taking a job that pays less, is likely to reduce the amount you'll receive someday from Social Security.

To decide when to take your Social Security, you need to assess your financial situation on an ongoing basis. Although you may qualify for benefits at age 62, you may be consulting or working part-time and don't need the money. When you reach the full retirement age at anywhere from 65 to 67, you can earn as much as you want without reducing your Social Security check.

If your income is too high, you may be taxed on your Social Security check. Therefore, you should consider the tax implications of working part-time. Unless you're well paid for part-time work, it may not be cost-effective to hold a job.

If your income is extremely low, look into the possibility of collecting Supplemental Security Income (SSI) benefits. This is a cash assistance program for the poor.

# CHAPTER 11

# Protecting your pension if you're lucky enough to have one

ACCORDING TO THE *PITTSBURGH POST-GAZETTE*, ONE ALLEGHENY COUNTY police officer made almost $112,000 in overtime in 2002 and was on track to earn about $202,000 in total compensation. As a result of the overtime, the officer's pension has increased significantly, and he'll receive a pension of over $98,000 if he retires in 2003. With cost of living increases, his pension will eventually exceed $100,000 per year.

The officer, and many others, were pulling double shifts as a result of security concerns after 9/11. County employees contribute 5 percent of their pay to the pension fund, and those earnings are matched dollar-for-dollar. Pensions in Allegheny County are based on the employee's two highest years of compensation in their last four years of employment. There is no cap on pensions in the county.

Most employees won't receive a pension when they retire, let alone

one that is more than $100,000 annually. The majority of people are lucky to leave with a basket of fruit and a nice card signed by all of their coworkers.

According to Horace B. Deets, the former executive director of AARP, retirement security was traditionally viewed as a three-legged stool. The three legs of the stool were Social Security, individual savings, and employer-provided pensions. Deets noted that the metaphor is outdated, because the traditional pension plan has been replaced at most companies by the 401(k).

If you discuss retirement with older people, you'll hear them talk about pension plans. If you discuss retirement with younger people, they'll be talking about 401(k) retirement savings plans. When the market was soaring and 401(k)s were riding high, many people weren't too concerned that their employers didn't offer a traditional pension. After the bear market that began in 2000, employees of any age would feel more secure with a pension. If you are entitled to a pension, you need to scrutinize the plan and make sure you're getting every penny you deserve.

## BACK TO BASICS

The pension is actually a defined benefit plan, and the 401(k) is a defined contribution plan. When you have a pension, you know how much you'll receive each month after a certain number of years of service. Your employer puts away the amount needed to pay yours and your coworkers' pensions.

Your odds of finding an employer with a defined benefit plan are about as good as finding an eight-track of your favorite recording artist. Only about 16 percent of employers offer defined benefit plans. Most offer their employees defined contribution plans. With the defined contribution plan, there are no guarantees as to how much will be paid at a specified age. The burden of investing money is on the employee, not the employer. Although the employer may match some or all of the employee's contribution, the plan does not specify how much the worker will receive in retirement benefits.

Pension plans either have a cliff vesting schedule or a graded vesting schedule. The cliff vesting schedule requires you to work the specified number of years required by the plan or you leave with no pension whatsoever. The graded vesting schedule is gradual, and some of your pension accrues at stipulated intervals. We saw earlier that the Economic Growth and Tax Relief Reconciliation Act of 2001 reduced the maximum time it takes for employer contributions to vest in 401(k) plans. That act only applies to employer matching contributions. It does not apply to non-matching contributions found in most traditional pension plans.

Most pension formulas put considerable emphasis on your compensation in the last few years of your employment. That's when the majority of workers get paid the most and increase the value of their pension. The pension estimate you get at earlier stages of your employment assumes you'll receive raises in pay over the years and will work another decade or two. If your career with that company doesn't go as planned, the pension might be far less than your expectations.

When you're ready to collect your pension, you'll need to choose between a single life annuity and a joint-and-survivor annuity. Another option might be a life annuity with a term certain. The pension plan may offer a "pop-up option," which allows the retiree who elects a survivor annuity to get back some of the reduction in pension if the designated beneficiary dies before the retiree.

Check whether your pension offers a survivor benefit. Your spouse may not be entitled to any portion of your pension if you haven't begun collecting and have not worked a specified number of years. In that case, it might be worthwhile to take a lump sum payout of your pension and roll it over into an IRA. Your spouse will then be the beneficiary of the IRA.

## LUMP SUM VERSUS MONTHLY CHECK

When it's time to retire, your pension administrator may offer you the chance to take a lump sum distribution of the amount owed. You should consider this if you'll make more with your money than by leaving it in the pension plan. However, there will be serious tax implications when taking a lump sum distribution, unless you roll the money over into an IRA.

This is an area where the traditional wisdom has changed as the result of the stock market debacle in 2000 through 2002. Previously, retirees thought they could do better with a lump sum payout of their pension. If you opted for the lump sum and invested it in recent years, you might have lost most of your pension.

The size of your lump sum is dependent upon many factors. Lump sum payments tend to go up when interest rates go down. Companies are now using more recent mortality tables, so pension calculations are based on longer life expectancies. As life expectancies get longer, lump sum payments go up.

If you choose to take a monthly check instead of a lump sum payment, you may be offered the option of receiving a higher monthly benefit in exchange for giving up your spouse's right to receive benefits upon your death. This is sometimes referred to as the pension max dilemma. Be wary of insurance agents who use the pension max dilemma to sell life insurance. They'll suggest that you take the higher monthly pension and then buy life insurance to protect your spouse. This isn't necessarily a good idea if your spouse likes the security of receiving your pension or may not invest the life insurance benefit wisely.

### TIPS FROM MARTIN NISSENBAUM, DIRECTOR, RETIREMENT PLANNING, ERNST & YOUNG

Take the lump sum if given a choice between the lump sum payout or the pension for life. The lump sum transferred to an IRA gives you more control over your investments, and you may earn more.

Most pension for life arrangements end at the death of the spouse, leaving nothing for the heirs.

Taking the monthly payout makes sense if you like the steady income and you're uncomfortable investing on your own.

## HONEY, I LOST MY PENSION

The bear market did more than just hurt your 401(k) retirement savings plan. It probably hurt your pension plan. When stock prices fall, a pension plan may have to change its assumptions regarding how much money it has to meet current and future obligations. The actuaries may determine that the pension plan is underfunded.

When a pension plan is underfunded, the company must shift assets to make up the shortfall. This may lead to lower profits, smaller dividends, and more debt. The end result is that the price of the company's stock may fall.

That's particularly bad news if you own stock in a company whose pension plan is underfunded. It's also a concern if you own too many shares of your employer's stock. As has been stressed before and will be repeated ad nauseum, you want to avoid putting too much of your 401(k) and other investments in your employer's stock.

Fortunately, your pension is insured by the Pension Benefit Guaranty Corporation (PBGC), an agency of the federal government. If you run into problems, contact the PBGC at 1200 K Street NW, Washington, DC 20005-4026, or call 202-326-4000. The website is www.pbgc.gov.

Jim McKay, a staff writer for the *Pittsburgh Post-Gazette*, reported on September 1, 2002, that bankrupt LTV Steel's pension plans were underfunded by $2.2 billion. The PBGC took over responsibility for the pension plans of roughly 82,000 former employees and retirees. The PBGC's exposure is the largest in its nearly thirty-year history. If large companies keep going out of business, LTV won't hold that dubious record for long.

The PBGC sets a maximum benefit guarantee each year. For pension plans that ended in 2002, the guarantee is $42,954.60 per year for a worker who retires at age 65. There is a lower guarantee if the worker collects benefits before age 65 or the pension covers another survivor or beneficiary. Therefore, if you're an extremely well-paid employee who's expecting a pension above that amount, some of your pension is at risk. 401(k) plans are not guaranteed, even though they're technically a pension.

If you've job-hopped throughout your career, you may be overlooking a small pension from a former employer. To find out if you've overlooked pension benefits from some period of employment, the PBGC operates a search service. Go to www.pbgc.gov and look for the pension search prompt. You'll need to type in your last name and Social Security number to see if there's a match.

Pensions are frequently divided up during a divorce. Even if retirement is years away, this is an extremely important issue to resolve. The Qualified Domestic Relations Order (QDRO) authorizes the plan administrator to make the appropriate distribution of a spouse's share of a pension and 401(k).

Because women frequently take time off from their career to raise a family, they lose the ability to build their own pension. The U.S. Department of Labor offers free guides on what women need to know about their pension rights. They can be obtained by calling 1-800-998-7542. Another resource is the Women's Institute for a Secure Retirement (WISER). The Web address is www.wiser.heinz.

## ADDITIONAL SOURCES OF PENSION ADVICE AND HELP

The American Academy of Actuaries: www.actuary.org

National Pension Lawyers Network: www.pensionaction.org

The Pension Rights Center: www.pensionrights.org

Pension and Welfare Benefits Administration: www.dol.gov .pwba

## CASH BALANCE PENSION PLANS

Even if your company offers a pension, the rules are changing. Beginning in the early 1980s, many companies switched from defined benefit plans to cash balance pensions. Generally, these cash balance pension plans save money for the employer.

Cash balance pension plans are a type of defined benefit plan, but with a different twist. With the traditional defined benefit plan, your pension is based on your age, salary, and years of service. With the traditional pension, your benefits grow significantly at later stages of your career. With cash balance pension plans, your pension grows gradually throughout your career.

When a company switches to a cash balance pension plan, older workers lose out on the big boost in their pension that occurs late in their career. As a result, these plans have been criticized as discriminating against older workers. Some older workers have joined together to fight their employer's switch to a cash balance pension plan. For example, older IBM workers successfully fought the company's attempt to change their pension plan.

Cash balance pensions are said to be more attractive to younger workers, because they are portable. They are easier to administer and offer younger workers more flexibility. Nevertheless, the Department of Labor's Office of Inspector General examined sixty cash balance pensions and found many early retirees were shortchanged.

The Treasury Department proposed rules in December 2002 that allow employers to convert their current pension benefit to a cash balance plan, as long as certain requirements are met. To comply with these rules, each participant must receive the fair present value of the pension at the time of conversion or the cash balance amount, whichever is greater. AARP and other organizations are fighting the new rules.

## PHASED RETIREMENT

The transition to retirement might be easier if more companies accept the concept of phased retirement. Phased retirement allows employees to work fewer hours during the period leading up to full retirement. Many universities now offer phased retirement to professors. Outside of the university setting, very few companies make phased retirement available to their employees. Phased retirement might take the form of part-time employment, job sharing, or a formally structured program.

There are currently disincentives that discourage phased retirement. For example, if a company's pension benefit is based on earnings during the last three years of employment, virtually no employees will agree to a reduction of hours during that time frame. More would be willing to participate if their pension were calculated using the three highest paid years of employment.

Phased retirement may find growing acceptance among companies that need to retain the expertise of their older workers. They are more likely to stay on if the new work arrangement doesn't impact their pension or other benefits. Phased retirement may also be the answer for workers who want to protect their retirement, but don't want to keep working full-time forever.

## PROTECTION TIPS

For most workers, a pension won't be part of their blueprint for retirement. If you don't have a pension coming your way, it's even more important that you save aggressively for retirement and invest knowledgeably. A fixed annuity can provide that guaranteed stream of income that you're missing if you don't receive a pension. Annuities can provide a lifetime income for you and a loved one.

No matter how old you are, you need to study your pension plan. Along with your employee handbook, study the Summary Plan Description that the company is obligated to provide. Watch out for any changes that may be implemented, such as a conversion to a cash balance pension plan.

Make sure you understand how your pension is calculated. Some plans refer to "Social Security integration," which means your benefit may be reduced to some degree by your Social Security check. If you believe you're being shortchanged in your lump sum payout or monthly benefit, you should have an actuary double-check the calculations.

You normally must work a specified number of weeks and hours in a year to get credit for it in your pension. Often, you must work at least 1,000 hours, or roughly twenty-five weeks.

Before handing in your notice, see if you're close to a pension milestone and decide if it's worth sticking around for a little longer at the company. If you're let go when you're close to a pension milestone, negotiate for a termination date that allows you to reach that important date.

# CHAPTER 12

# Protecting your retirement

# from a job loss

THE BANKRUPTCY OF LTV STEEL HAMMERED WORKERS WITH A FLURRY OF blows. For many workers, there was no sixty-day notice of the plant's closing as required by law. The workers received no severance pay, nor were they paid for their unused vacation time. Their defined benefit plan, as well as their 401(k) defined contribution plan, were disrupted by the bankruptcy proceedings. Many workers were left scrambling for alternative health insurance plans, and some were unable to find any.

Ideally, you'll have the choice of when to retire. Sometimes, however, you'll be forced to leave your job long before you're ready, psychologically or economically, to retire. To protect your retirement from a job loss, you need to know your legal options, as well as the tax laws affecting 401(k) distributions.

## The Impact of Premature
## Retirement on Your 401(k)

In Chapters 10 and 11, we looked at the adverse impact that a job loss can have on your Social Security and your pension. A job loss, especially as you're nearing retirement, can do serious damage to your retirement savings plan.

As you near retirement age, you should be contributing more to retirement accounts. The cap on contributions to a 401(k) is getting higher each year. Furthermore, if you're age 50 or older, you can make catch-up contributions to your 401(k). If you lose your job at this stage of life, however, you won't even make your normal contributions. You'll miss out on years of compounded growth in this tax-sheltered account.

It's bad enough that you're not putting money in your 401(k). You also may need to take money out. If you need the money, 59½ is the magic age when you can withdraw money without fear of the 10 percent premature distribution penalty. There is also an exception in place if you're age 55 or older and terminated from service. You may be able to withdraw money from your 401(k) without incurring a penalty. This exception was carved out to help laid-off workers in their mid-to-late fifties who had difficulty finding new jobs.

Although the money you take from a 401(k) isn't subject to a penalty, you'll pay taxes at your current income tax rate. One option is to have your employer split the 401(k). You might want to take enough cash to tide you over until age 59½ and put the rest directly into an IRA.

You might be in serious trouble if you're fired or laid off and you've borrowed money from your 401(k) retirement savings plan. If you're laid off, your loan comes due immediately. If the loan isn't repaid, it is viewed as an early withdrawal. To avoid taxes, the entire amount must be rolled over into an IRA.

Different rules apply if you make a hardship withdrawal from your 401(k). A hardship withdrawal is not a loan. Hardship withdrawals are only permitted if you can prove an immediate financial need, such as college expenses, a mortgage, or significant medical bills, or to avoid eviction. Employers are required to verify your need for a hardship withdrawal, and the amount withdrawn can't be greater than your need. The hardship withdrawal is taxed, and you'll pay a 10 percent early withdrawal penalty if you're younger than 59½.

Even if you haven't borrowed money from your 401(k), you may have a bigger problem. Many employees invest too much of their 401(k) money in their employer's stock, and that's extremely dangerous. According to BankruptcyData.com, 257 public companies filed for Chapter 11 bankruptcy in 2001. In 2002, 186 companies filed for bankruptcy, but the value of those filings was a record $368 billion. Among the companies that filed for bankruptcy were WorldCom Inc., Global Crossing Ltd., Conseco Inc., Adelphia Communications Inc., and UAL Corp.

When too much of your 401(k) plan is tied up in your employer's stock and the company has financial problems, you risk losing a good chunk of your retirement savings and your job. On top of those problems, you may wind up with a file drawer filled with worthless stock options.

Fortunately, although 401(k) plans are not insured, they are protected by federal law. The assets in 401(k) plans are held separately from the employer's assets. Nevertheless, if a bankrupt company terminates its 401(k) plan, the dispersal of assets to employees doesn't always go smoothly. Plan sponsors are required to have a fidelity bond, but that doesn't mean they will, just as there are people riding around without auto insurance.

At a film company in Crafton, Pennsylvania, a woman's employer deducted money from her paycheck to repay her 401(k) loan. However, her employer did not forward her loan payments to the 401(k) plan administrator. Not long afterwards, the employer's bank foreclosed on the loan that was keeping the company afloat. When the employer closed its doors, the plan administrator advised her that she must either pay the full loan back or allow it to default, resulting in taxes and a 10 percent premature distribution penalty.

This woman faced the loss of her loan payments that the employer didn't forward to the plan administrator. She may also owe taxes on the loan, since it's viewed as a distribution if not repaid. In addition, she may owe a 10 percent tax penalty on the distribution. Finally, she's no longer receiving a paycheck.

## SEVERANCE PAY

According to Standard & Poor's, workers age 45 and older account for 25 percent of unemployment, compared to 19 percent in 1991. Older workers also remain unemployed for longer than younger workers. Whereas younger workers will have time to rebuild their retirement savings, older employees may have irreparable damage done to their 401(k)s, Social Security, and pensions.

To protect your retirement, you need to be prepared for a job loss. Start reading your employee handbook, so you'll know how much severance pay you can count on getting. Often, when companies merge, there is a great deal of confusion regarding how much severance pay is owed. In many cases, the employer may have no contractual obligation to provide severance pay. As we saw with WorldCom and other corporate bankruptcies, companies won't always shell out severance pay in a lump sum. When severance pay is paid out in installments, you're in danger that the company will declare bankruptcy and your checks will stop coming.

Even if there is no contractual obligation to provide severance pay, some employers will offer it anyway but will require a *quid pro quo*. An employer may require you to sign away your legal rights in exchange for severance pay. A condition of getting the money is that you sign a document promising not to sue.

Often, these lawsuit waivers go hand in hand with an early retirement incentive package. They protect the company from lawsuits alleging age discrimination. The Older Workers Benefit Protection Act of 1990 stipulates that lawsuit waivers must be voluntary and written in understandable language. You must be given twenty-one days to consider the waiver if it's made to you as an individual. If an offer of severance pay in exchange for a lawsuit waiver is made to a group of employees, you have forty-five days to consider it.

Even after you sign a lawsuit waiver in exchange for severance pay, you may still have some rights because of the Older Workers Benefit Protection Act. You must be allowed seven days to revoke the waiver after accepting the offer of severance pay. If federal law isn't adhered to, you can still sue and may be allowed to keep your severance pay until the litigation is over. Before signing any legal document, you may wish to consult with an attorney.

Even if you feel your job is secure, be prepared for the day when you might get your pink slip, and be ready to negotiate your severance package. If you're not entitled to severance pay, ask for it anyway. If you're offered severance pay, negotiate for more.

The employer may be willing to keep you on the payroll for a few extra weeks, especially if you're a well-liked employee and you offer a business justification for postponing your last day. You might be able to squeeze out a few more weeks on the payroll by offering to finish a big project you've been working on or to train the coworker who will be assuming your duties.

Put together a wish list of realistic perks that your employer might be willing to relinquish as part of your severance package. If you're near a milestone such as 401(k) or stock option vesting, ask if you can postpone your last day until after that event occurs.

Start looking for alternative benefits. As we'll see in Chapter 13, COBRA is an expensive way to buy health insurance. Look for an individual policy that might be offered from the Blue Cross/Blue Shield in your area. If you belong to an organization, there may be group policies available.

If you're really desperate, you can withdraw money from your IRA to pay health insurance premiums. You won't pay a premature distribution penalty if you withdraw money to pay health insurance premiums for yourself, your spouse, and/or your dependents. You will, however, pay a penalty unless you meet each and every one of the following conditions:

1. You lost your job.
2. For twelve or more consecutive weeks, you received unemployment compensation.
3. The withdrawal or withdrawals are made during the year you received unemployment benefits or during the following year.
4. The withdrawals are made no later than sixty days after you're employed again.

If you meet all of these conditions, you won't pay the 10 percent penalty, but you'll pay income taxes on the amount withdrawn. If you have a Roth IRA, you'll lose out on tax-free withdrawals. You're also sacrificing future growth to pay current expenses.

## PENALTY-FREE WITHDRAWALS FROM YOUR IRA TO PAY MEDICAL BILLS

Just as you can use your IRA in certain situations to help pay for the cost of health insurance, you can also tap your IRA to pay for medical expenses. Naturally, you can't make a penalty-free withdrawal for every doctor visit. The medical expenses must not have been covered by insurance and must exceed 7.5 percent of your adjusted gross income. This 7.5 percent figure should sound familiar because it's the same percentage used on the 1040 form to calculate whether medical expenses are deductible. Similarly, only medical expenses above 7.5 percent qualify if you're hoping to take a penalty-free withdrawal from your IRA.

For readers who aren't accountants, here's how it works. Let's say you're younger than age 59½ and have $10,000 in medical bills that weren't covered by insurance. If your adjusted gross income (AGI) is $50,000, you multiply 7.5 percent times your AGI. The figure you should come up with is $3,750. Therefore, since the difference between $10,000 and $3,750 is $6,250, you may make a penalty-free withdrawal of $6,250 from your IRA if the money is used to pay those medical bills. If you withdraw $10,000 from your IRA to pay all of your medical bills, $3,750 will be subject to a premature distribution penalty.

Once again, tapping your IRA before age 59 ½ is not a good idea, even if you don't pay a penalty. You'll cut drastically into your savings for retirement. Furthermore, if you have a Roth IRA, you'll pay taxes on the withdrawal, which defeats the purpose of that account. If you wait until age 59 ½, and the account has been open for at least five years, Roth IRA withdrawals will be tax-free.

Before tapping an IRA to pay for health insurance or medical bills, look to see if there are any other possible options. At a minimum, try to negotiate with medical providers to see if they will accept a lower amount to satisfy their bills.

## PROTECTION TIPS

Your blueprint to protect and rebuild your retirement shouldn't go out the window if you lose your job. You should always have a fallback plan if you suspect your job is in jeopardy. You might be forced to retire prematurely if your employer runs into financial problems or is downsizing employees.

You need to create contingency plans in case your retirement strategy is undermined by a job loss. Make sure any loans against your 401(k) are paid off, since they'll come due upon termination, and failing to pay them back will be viewed as a premature distribution.

One option is to shift to more conservative investments if your job is in jeopardy. Make sure your portfolio is not overloaded with company stock.

Use your emergency fund and ready cash before tapping tax-sheltered retirement accounts. IRAs and 401(k)s grow much faster than taxable accounts. The longer you can avoid touching tax-sheltered accounts, the better off you'll be.

If you're on the verge of losing your job, do some tax planning. Where possible, push some of your income into next year when your tax bracket is likely to be lower. Take as many of your deductions this year when they'll do you more good.

# CHAPTER 13

# Protecting your retirement
# with insurance

MICKEY MANTLE ONCE SAID, "IF I HAD KNOWN I WAS GOING TO LIVE THIS long, I would have taken better care of myself." Too bad Mantle didn't give the same advice to Keith Richards of the Rolling Stones. Hopefully, your lifestyle doesn't include keeping lit cigarettes in between the strings of your guitar while playing licks like Keith does.

Even if you were never into sex, drugs, and rock 'n' roll, there are no guarantees of good health. Just as bad investments can mess up your plans for retirement, a medical problem, an accident, or the deterioration of your health can do as much damage or more. There also might be a special someone who depends upon your income for retirement. Therefore, it's imperative that you have the right insurance to protect your retirement.

## HEALTH INSURANCE

You don't need a lecture on the importance of having a good health insurance policy. Hopefully, you're not one of the 41.2 million Americans who, according to the Census Bureau, lack health insurance.

In 2001, the number of uninsured Americans increased by 1.4 million. Much of the increase was attributed to the weak economy and rising health care costs. Many employers who once used good health care benefits to attract employees are dropping coverage or passing on more of the expense to their workers. When health insurance becomes more expensive, more workers opt to drop the coverage.

Even people who are insured may not have enough coverage. Many retirees have limited or no coverage for prescription drugs. Even among working people, health insurance premiums, deductibles, and copayments take a big bite out of their paycheck and, consequently, they may decide to forgo treatment and medication to avoid paying their share of the costs. As an example, a study published in the *Journal of the American Medical Association* found that the average number of filled prescriptions declined as out-of-pocket expenses increased.

One of the most disturbing trends in recent years is the number of companies who are cutting back on health insurance benefits for retirees. The Summary Plan Description (SPD) from your employer may include specific language that reserves the company's right to change the plan. If this is the case, the employer may eliminate or reduce your health insurance benefits in retirement. Some companies are making it clear from the first day of employment that health insurance will not be included in an employee's retirement package.

Retirees have few options when their health insurance expenses rise, especially those who are on a fixed income. Furthermore, retirees who aren't eligible for Medicare will have difficulty finding health insurance coverage from sources other than their employer. Their age and their health may work against them as they seek alternative coverage.

COBRA won't help much if you're too young to qualify for Medicare. First of all, it's only a temporary solution. Unless there are special circumstances, you only qualify for eighteen months of coverage. It's also extremely expensive. The cost of group coverage through employers has gone up significantly. According to the Kaiser Family Foundation, you'll pay almost $663 per month for family coverage, plus a 2 percent administrative charge, to continue your coverage under COBRA. And you aren't entitled to the employer's contribution. The cost of HMO coverage might be slightly less.

Start by checking the Blue Cross/Blue Shield in your area. It may offer health insurance programs for people in your situation. Your state's insurance department may know of policies that are available. You should also consider a group health insurance policy through an organization to which you belong.

Make sure the policy is guaranteed renewable, no matter what your health is at the time of renewal. To keep the cost down, select as high a deductible as you can afford. Contact regulators in your state to be sure the company offering the policy is reliable and in good standing.

If you like the idea of working in retirement, look for a part-time job that offers health insurance benefits. Usually, you're required to work a specified number of hours each week to be eligible for health insurance benefits.

Another possibility is to start your own small business. Beginning in 2003, if you're self-employed, you can usually deduct 100 percent of your health insurance premiums. Otherwise, you can only deduct health insurance premiums as a miscellaneous deduction, and they must exceed 7.5 percent of your adjusted gross income to do you any good on your tax return.

## MEDICARE AND COVERAGE
## TO SUPPLEMENT MEDICARE

To protect your retirement against the risk of illness, you need to find out what happens to your current coverage when you're eligible for Medicare. Frequently, Medicare becomes your primary insurance. Normally, any coverage from your former employer becomes secondary and picks up the expenses that Medicare doesn't cover.

Medicare by itself is not adequate coverage for most retirees. There are many gaps in the coverage provided by Medicare. You may need coverage over and above traditional Medicare to protect your retirement nest egg.

## Medicare supplemental policies

You can enhance your protection with a Medicare supplement, commonly known as a Medigap policy. There are ten standard Medicare supplemental policies, identified by letters A to J. As you move down the alphabet, the policies offer more coverage, such as reimbursement for prescriptions. Because policies are standardized, you get the same coverage if you buy the same letter policy from any insurer. Although the policies are standard, rates can vary from company to company.

Not every type of Medigap policy will be offered in your state. The insurance department in your state should provide information on the companies licensed to sell policies. The state insurance department may also provide information on which companies are the strongest financially.

## Medicare + choice

An alternative to the original Medicare Plan is privately sold insurance. You sign up for a Medicare + Choice plan, sometimes referred to as Medicare C. These plans are usually managed care plans, which is why they're sometimes called Medicare HMOs (Health Maintenance Organizations) or Medicare PPOs (Preferred Provider Organizations).

Medicare HMOs are managed care plans that require enrollees to use a specific provider network. HMOs were initially promoted as a way for seniors to receive drug benefits and other coverage not provided by the original Medicare. For roughly the same cost as the original Medicare, the Medicare HMO enrollee got some of the extra coverage found in a Medigap policy.

In recent years, however, many Medicare HMOs reduced their benefits, increased their premiums, and a number of companies terminated their coverage. This termination forced enrollees to switch to another Medicare HMO or return to the original Medicare. According to the November 2002 issue of *AARP Bulletin*, nearly 217,000 Medicare beneficiaries were dropped by their HMO in 2002.

In some areas, Medicare PPOs are available. The PPO allows the enrollee to go directly to specialists without a referral from the primary care physician. The enrollee may also go to an out-of-network provider in exchange for a higher copayment. The PPO may offer a modest amount of coverage for prescription drugs. There is a smaller copayment for visits to providers within the network.

## DO I NEED LONG-TERM CARE INSURANCE?

When you sit down with agents selling long-term care insurance, they'll quote you statistics on why you need a policy. To persuade you to buy long-term car insurance, the agent will say you have a one in eighty chance of using your homeowners policy. She will say there is a one in forty chance you'll need your auto policy. The agent may say there's a 60 percent chance you'll be in a nursing home at some point after age 65, according to the Department of Health and Human Services, however, 43 percent of all Americans will need long-term care at some point in their lives, but that doesn't mean they'll require it for an extended period.

The agent will also offer statistics dealing with the cost of long-term care. According to a study from the MetLife Mature Market Institute, the average cost of a nursing home in the United States is $168 per day for a private room and the tab may be $300 or more in some areas. Assisted living costs an average of $2,159 per month, and you'll pay more at an assisted-living facility if you need additional care. Home health care costs an average of ninety dollars per day.

The average stay in a nursing home is about two-and-a-half years. Furthermore, long-term care costs are expected to triple in twenty years. If you do the math, it isn't hard to see that you'll need a lot of money if you or a loved one needs long-term care.

Whether you have Medicare, a Medicare supplement, or belong to a Medicare HMO or PPO, there's one thing for sure. Your retirement is still threatened by the risk of needing long-term care. Many people incorrectly assume that long-term care expenses are covered by Medicare or some variation thereof. Even if you're not retired and have a comprehensive health insurance policy, you most likely have inadequate coverage for long-term care expenses. Therefore, a long-term care policy is worth considering.

Without insurance, long-term care expenses can eat up a large chunk of your paycheck or your retirement income. The best long-term care policies can keep you out of a nursing home, because they pay for assisted living, home health care, homemaker services, and adult day care. A policy might even pay for house modifications like a wheelchair ramp, so the person in need of care can stay at home for as long as possible. The alternative plan of care gives the insurer the discretion to authorize home modifications and other services that aren't specifically outlined in the policy.

## Shopping for a long-term care policy

Buying a tax-qualified long-term care policy is a way to ensure that the benefits eligibility trigger, and other features, meet the standards established by the government. To collect on a tax-qualified policy, you must be unable to perform two or more activities of daily living, such as dressing or bathing, without substantial help from another person for at least ninety days. If you don't meet that test, you can still qualify for benefits if you're cognitively impaired and need substantial supervision to protect your health and safety.

Although tax-qualified policies have certain features in common, long-term care policies differ from company to company. Therefore, you must scrutinize the policy to be sure it contains the coverage you need. A shortcut is to read the outline of coverage that describes the benefits and exclusions in the policy. Ask a friend, relative, or adviser you trust for help.

A policy is worthless without coverage for devastating mental conditions like Alzheimer's disease. Although Alzheimer's disease should be covered without restriction, there will be exclusions for other types of mental problems. The long-term care policy won't normally cover personality disorders or nervous conditions.

Make sure you're getting a guaranteed renewable policy that can be renewed at your option, regardless of your health at the time. Nevertheless, guaranteed renewable doesn't mean that the premium will always remain the same. Your premium may be increased if the state insurance department approves a rate hike for everyone with the same policy who is in the same classification as you. Be sure you can afford the premium if it goes up significantly.

Thousands of home health care policyholders in Florida got bad news in August 2002. They received a letter advising them of a 45 percent rate hike by Conseco Senior Health Insurance Co. The price hike was said to be unrelated to the parent company's financial troubles.

When your long-term care insurer raises its rates, you have few options. You might find it difficult to qualify for a policy at another long-term care insurer. Furthermore, the rates at a new insurance company are likely to be high, because you're older than when you first applied for coverage. You might be forced to drop your coverage at an age when you need it most.

Be sure to buy adequate benefits at an affordable price. Compare the daily benefit of the policy with the typical long-term care charges in your area. You must also select the right benefit period, which governs how long benefits will be paid. A benefit period can last anywhere from one year to the lifetime of the policyholder.

A long-term care policy isn't going to do you much good twenty years from now if your benefit is the same as it is today. Inflation riders add significantly to the price of a policy, but help it keep pace with the escalating cost of long-term care. If you've waited until your mid-to-late seventies to buy a policy, buying inflation protection isn't as important. If you're in your fifties, inflation protection is extremely important.

## Cutting costs

One way to cut the cost of a long-term care policy is by agreeing to a longer elimination period, which is how long you must wait for benefits to begin. A waiting period of ninety days or longer can cut your premium significantly, but you may run up a significant bill for long-term care in the interim. At $150 per day for long-term care, ninety days hits you in the wallet for $13,500, which is a far cry from a $500 deductible on your auto insurance.

With most long-term care policies, the premium is based in part on your age at the time of purchase, and you may not qualify at all if you're in poor health. Sixty is about the time you should decide whether or not to buy a long-term care policy. Nevertheless, consider buying it sooner if you can get an inexpensive policy through your employer or if you are worried about your health deteriorating.

Group policies offer a less expensive way to insure against the risk of needing long-term care. The federal government recently unveiled coverage for current employees and retirees. Qualified relatives of the federal employee may also be entitled to purchase the group coverage.

## Before You Buy a Long-Term Care Policy

Before buying a long-term care policy, find out if there are programs in your state to help you evaluate the coverage. Your state insurance department might offer this service or will know who can help. Another source of information is the Eldercare Locator, sponsored by the Administration on Aging, U.S. Department of Health and Human Services. You can reach their offices by calling 1-800-677-1116.

Make sure you check the financial strength of the long-term care insurer writing the policy. Find out the company's ratings from A.M. Best (www.ambest.com), Standard & Poor's (www.standardandpoors.com), Moody's Investors Service (www.moodys.com), and Weiss Ratings Inc. (www.weissratings.com). Your state's insurance department may also have information about the financial stability of the company offering the coverage.

An attorney who specializes in elder law or a financial planner might be able to help you with long-term care issues. Lawyer referrals are available through the National Academy of Elder Law Attorneys at www .naela.org. We'll look at how to choose a financial planner in Chapter 16.

Some financial planners believe you can self-insure against the risk of needing long-term care. If your income is large enough, you can pay long-term care expenses out of your own pocket. Another possibility is to buy a deferred annuity that pays for long-term care expenses if the need arises. You won't get the same quality of coverage as you will with long-term care insurance, but it might be an alternative for someone who doesn't qualify to buy a long-term care policy.

**SEPARATING FACT FROM FICTION IN A LONG-TERM CARE POLICY**

Don't let the agent lead you to believe that the alternative plan of care language covers any and every situation where care is needed.

Don't let the agent oversell you on the tax deduction for buying a tax-qualified policy. Premiums are only partially deductible and only if your medical expenses exceed 7.5 percent of your adjusted gross income. Insurers are lobbying for better tax breaks for people buying long-term care policies.

Approval of a policy by the state insurance department doesn't mean the government is endorsing the company. State approval only means the policy has met the minimum standards required by law. Check out whether the agent selling the policy is licensed and if there have been complaints against him with the state insurance department.

## DISABILITY INSURANCE

A disability can put a halt to your retirement planning. You face more than a 40 percent chance of being disabled for longer than ninety days between age 30 and age 65. The risk of becoming disabled is greater than the risk of dying at certain ages. If you become disabled, you'll lose the ability to put away money for retirement for a short time or an extended period. You'll also lose the ability to put away money in your checking account to cover your current bills.

Although an agent is more than happy to sell you a disability insurance policy, the insurer doesn't want you to buy too much coverage. If your disability checks are too high, you may like cashing them more than working. The insurance company wants you to have a financial incentive to return to work. Most insurers will limit the policy you buy to 60 percent to 70 percent of your gross income.

The group policy you get through your employer is usually inadequate. It may only provide short-term coverage. If your employer pays the premium, the benefits are taxable.

An individual disability policy is often worth the extra cost. The benefits are tax-free if you paid the premium. The definition of disability is likely to be more in your favor. You can customize the coverage and easily add cost-of-living riders. Since an extended disability will do damage to your retirement savings program, some companies offer policy enhancements that can bolster your retirement nest egg.

You can save money on disability insurance by extending the waiting period for benefits to begin. As we saw with long-term care insurance, a ninety-day waiting period will cut your cost significantly. The waiting period is much like the deductible on other insurance policies. You can also save money by buying a group disability policy through a trade group or professional organization to which you belong.

## PROTECTING YOUR LIFE INSURANCE AND OTHER BENEFITS

When you retire, you may be losing other important insurance benefits. Most employees obtain group life insurance through work. In theory, you have little need for life insurance as you get older, but that's not necessarily the case. For example, it's not uncommon for retirees to have children or grandchildren who depend upon them for support.

Your spouse or life partner may lose considerable income if you pass away. Your husband or wife's income from Social Security may be much less. If you die, your spouse may face a cut in your pension or no pension whatsoever. In Chapter 11, we discussed the pension max issue. The worker who is retiring takes a higher pension but the surviving spouse gives up his or her benefit. To make up for the loss of a pension, the retiree buys life insurance to protect the spouse.

If you're still working, ask your employee benefits department about the life insurance you're entitled to upon retirement. Find out if the policy can be converted and the price. If you're healthy, you might be better off buying an individual policy.

If you know that you'll need life insurance in retirement, look into buying a policy now. Even if you're older, you might be able to find a reasonably priced term insurance policy that is guaranteed renewable. The life insurer must renew your policy, even if your health deteriorates. With term life insurance, you're buying pure protection, not a lot of extras.

You can buy a term life insurance policy that guarantees a premium for a stated number of years. You can lock in a guaranteed rate for five, ten, fifteen, twenty, or even thirty years. A premium guaranteed for twenty years will be more expensive than one guaranteed for five years or one year. A $100,000 twenty-year-level premium policy for a healthy 50-year-old woman costs in the neighborhood of twenty dollars per month.

The policy should be guaranteed renewable. It should permit you to renew regardless of your health at the time of renewal. The policy may also offer a guaranteed conversion feature. If it does, you can convert the term policy to a permanent life insurance policy such as whole life. The younger you are at the time of conversion, the lower your premiums will be.

Whole life provides insurance coverage and a savings component. The policy builds cash value within it. You can borrow against the cash value without any tax consequences. The premium, which is based on your age and health at the time of purchase, stays the same. Some whole life policies offer an accelerated death benefit. Normally, this feature entitles you to some or all of your death benefit if you become terminally ill or need long-term care.

Shop around for the best price on a term policy. Try Quotesmith .com (www.quotesmith.com; 1-800-556-9393), AccuTerm (www.accu term.com; 1-888-807-5792), Compulife (www.term4life.com), and other websites that compare the price of policies. Compare an individual policy with group insurance through an organization or group to which you belong. You can also get unbiased information about insurance at Glenn Daily's website (www.glenndaily.com).

Make sure the bear market hasn't undermined the coverage you already have now. With variable life insurance, for example, a portion of your premium is invested. Your investment gains might be used to increase your coverage or offset some of the premium. If the investment account is losing money, however, there may not be enough money to sustain the policy.

## PROTECTION TIPS

The most comprehensive blueprint for protecting your retirement is incomplete without insurance. Inadequate insurance coverage can wipe out years of savings and can ravage your plans for retirement.

The best time to buy insurance is before you need it. If your job situation is tenuous, look for a permanent health insurance policy. It might be less expensive than COBRA, and you won't lose the policy after eighteen months. Buy any other policies you need while you're relatively young and healthy. Don't buy any insurance without checking out the agent and the company through your state's insurance department.

If you buy long-term care insurance by age 60, the policy should be affordable. Long-term care coverage can give you alternatives to spending your final days in a nursing home. Remember that Medicare and Medicare supplemental policies offer little coverage for long-term care.

Whether you buy a long-term care policy or not, look for a living situation that will allow you to stay in your home as you age. One of the newest trends in homebuilding is to facilitate aging in place. Homes are being built with features that might enable the owners to live there for the rest of their lives. Doorways are wider in case the owner needs a wheelchair someday and there are few steps, as well as master bedrooms on the ground floor. You increase the chances of staying in your home forever by modifying the structure to accommodate the physical limitations that sometimes come with age.

Although it is generally true that your need for life insurance diminishes with age, many people will still need a policy after they retire. If your pension ends at the death of your spouse, life insurance can be used to make up the deficit. Look for a permanent whole life policy, or a level term life insurance plan that will cover you for ten to thirty years. If you buy it in your late forties or early fifties, the cost should not be exorbitant. Shop around for the best price on a policy from a reliable company.

# CHAPTER 14

# Protecting your retirement from taxes

If your eyes glaze over at the mere mention of taxes, make a strong pot of coffee. Protecting your retirement from taxes is one of the most important things you can do.

Many retirees mistakenly presume they'll be in a much lower tax bracket in retirement. Sidney Weinman, a tax attorney in New York City, has called it "The Biggest Retirement Myth." If in spite of the recent bear market you're sitting on a huge nest egg, your income in retirement might be significant, and you will find yourself in one of the highest tax brackets.

It's important that you understand the impact of taxes on your retirement planning. You might think you're sitting pretty with $1 million in a 401(k) or a traditional IRA. But that $1 million doesn't look so huge if you consider that you'll lose thirty or forty dollars in federal and state taxes on every $100 you withdraw.

You can protect your retirement by taking full advantage of tax-sheltered accounts, as well as tax-advantaged investments. You also need to minimize the impact of taxes on your Social Security benefits.

## BACK TO BASICS

For all that's changed in the tax laws, the magical age of 59½ still remains for now. That's the age when you can normally access your retirement accounts without paying a tax penalty. If you're younger than 59½, you'll usually pay a 10 percent tax penalty on withdrawals, as well as any taxes owed on the money withdrawn. As we saw earlier, there are instances where a penalty is not owed, even if you're younger than age 59½.

### 72(t) withdrawals

Whether you're withdrawing from a 401(k) or IRA, you can use a 72(t) withdrawal to avoid the 10 percent tax penalty. Under Section 72(t) of the Internal Revenue Code, you are permitted to take substantially equal payments from your IRA based on your life expectancy. The withdrawals must be taken each year for at least five years or until age 59½, whichever is longer.

If you want to withdraw money before age 59½, the 72(t) withdrawal is helpful, but it has its limitations. Since the withdrawals are based on your life expectancy, the amount you may withdraw is relatively small. Also, Section 72(t) forces you to keep making withdrawals, even if you don't need the money.

Let's say you're age 50 and begin taking substantially equal payments from your retirement account. You must keep making withdrawals until you're age 59½ or you'll pay a penalty. If you're 56 and begin taking substantially equal payments from your retirement account, the withdrawals must continue until age 61, since that's the five-year minimum.

Once you begin 72(t) distributions, you must keep making them, although the IRS recently said you can readjust your withdrawal formula. You may win the lottery or inherit a fortune, but you still must make your withdrawals. Another problem with 72(t) withdrawals is that they increase the chances that you'll exhaust your nest egg prematurely. To protect your nest egg, you should be building your retirement accounts before age 59½, not withdrawing from them.

It should also be noted that 72(t) withdrawals defeat the purpose of a Roth IRA. When you take substantially equal payments from your Roth IRA before age 59½, you avoid the 10 percent penalty on premature distributions, but you'll pay taxes on the money taken out. You lose the glorious feature of a Roth IRA, which is that qualified withdrawals are tax-free.

## THE TAX ADVANTAGES OF THE ROTH IRA

Even if you are in a lower bracket in retirement, it will go a lot farther if you can minimize your tax bite. We looked earlier at the tax advantages of a Roth IRA. If you play by the rules, your withdrawals will be tax-free. You can also withdraw your contributions at any time for any reason and without tax consequences.

Roth IRAs came along too late for most readers. They were created by the Taxpayer Relief Act of 1997, and came into being on January 1, 1998. Most readers have the bulk of their retirement savings in traditional IRAs and 401(k)s, which allow you to defer taxes on the earnings. You'll pay taxes when you withdraw the funds.

One strategy is to convert your traditional IRA to a Roth IRA. This might be a particularly good idea if the assets in your IRA are lower in value, because of stock market setbacks. You can convert a traditional IRA to a Roth IRA if your modified adjusted gross income is not more than $100,000. The income restriction doesn't include the amount to be converted. You're not permitted to make this conversion if you're married and filing a separate return. You're also required to keep your money in the Roth IRA for five years after the conversion.

Since you're taxed right away on the amount converted, you might ask: Why should I convert a traditional IRA to a Roth IRA if I'm going to be taxed anyway? The answer is that you're paying taxes on the IRA before it grows further in value. Your tax bill now is far less than it will be years down the road.

Suppose you have $200,000 in a traditional IRA. Assuming an 8 percent rate of return, it will be worth $400,000 in about nine years. Since it is a traditional IRA, you will pay taxes on the entire $400,000 as it is withdrawn.

If you convert that traditional IRA to a Roth IRA, you'll pay taxes on the $200,000 that is in the account. From that point on, however, you will enjoy all of the benefits of a Roth IRA. Future withdrawals will be tax-free, even though the account has grown by $200,000 in value. You also won't face mandatory withdrawals at age 70$^1/_2$.

Consult with an accountant before converting your traditional IRA to a Roth IRA. You can also consult these websites for information: FinanCenter: www.financenter.com; Vanguard: www.vanguard.com; Roth IRA Advisor: www.Rothira-advisor.com. If you're receiving Social Security benefits, remember that the amount converted may increase the taxes you owe on your monthly check.

## PAYING TAXES ON YOUR SOCIAL SECURITY

If your Social Security check seems small after forty years in the workforce, you won't be thrilled about having to pay taxes on your benefits. Depending upon your income, you may have to pay taxes on up to 85 percent of your benefits. Whether you owe taxes depends on your combined income. Combined income is the sum of your adjusted gross income (AGI), in addition to your nontaxable interest, plus one-half of your Social Security benefits.

If you're filing a joint return, and your combined income is between $32,000 and $44,000, you may have to pay taxes on 50 percent of your benefits. When your combined income is higher than $44,000, you face income tax on up to 85 percent of your Social Security benefits.

If you file an individual return and your combined income is between $25,000 and $34,000, you may have to pay taxes on 50 percent of your Social Security check. When your combined income is higher than $34,000, up to 85 percent of your Social Security check is taxable.

## THE TAX ADVANTAGES OF SAVINGS BONDS

Savings bonds still represent a safe and reliable way to protect your retirement from taxes with virtually no risk. If you're nearing retirement age or are already there, you may own older savings bonds. Some may have stopped earning interest, so check with your bank or on the Internet at www.savingsbond.gov.

When you buy savings bonds, you may pay taxes on the interest yearly or wait until the bonds are redeemed. The interest from savings bonds is subject to federal tax, but is exempt from state and local taxes. Most people hold off on paying taxes until they redeem the bond. When a bond is cashed in, you'll pay taxes on all those years of deferred interest. Ideally, you'll be in a lower tax bracket at the time of redemption, but that isn't always the case.

To delay paying taxes and to generate income, you can exchange those older bonds for HH bonds. If you exchange a bond for an HH bond, you don't have to pay taxes on all the interest that has been deferred since its purchase. The interest paid in the past rolls over into the HH bond. With the HH bond, you only pay taxes on the interest paid out. The amount of interest carried over from the previous bond will be listed on the HH bond.

The interest is paid out every six months, so you're only going to get checks twice each year. To assure yourself a monthly check, you can convert some of your bonds each month to HH bonds. Then, each will reach the six-month mark in a different month and you'll receive a regular interest check.

You can't buy HH bonds with cash. They are only available in exchange for Series E, EE, and Series H bonds. Since HH bonds are sold in $500 increments, the value of bonds you're exchanging won't exactly match what you're buying. You are permitted to add money, so you reach the next $500 increment. You can also take money back and round down to the next lower $500 increment, but some or all of that money will be taxable.

You may be out of luck if you're trying to exchange very old bonds. If the bond is more than one year older than the date of final maturity, you cannot exchange it for an HH bond. Your only option is to redeem it and pay taxes on the interest.

Savings bonds can do more than just generate income in retirement. Certain savings bonds can be used to put away money for a child's education. If you're within the income limits at the time of redemption and the bond is cashed in to pay for qualified higher education expenses, your earnings will be tax-free.

## PROTECTION TIPS

Tax planning can make it easier to protect and rebuild your retirement. You can't base your blueprint for retirement on the assumption that you'll be in a lower tax bracket after you retire.

Building a large traditional IRA will help to secure your retirement, but each withdrawal will be subject to taxes. Consider converting your traditional IRA to a Roth IRA, especially if the value of your account is down. Although you'll pay taxes now, your future earnings will be tax-free.

Keep three to five years of living expenses in ready cash. The money should be in an account you can get at without causing yourself a tax problem. If you're relying on a traditional IRA or a 401(k) for ready cash, withdrawals may throw you into a higher tax bracket. Whenever you can, keep funds in tax-deferred accounts for as long as possible.

If your income is lower during a particular year, cash in some of those savings bonds that have been accruing interest for years and are nearing the time when they stop paying interest. Try to time your bond redemptions, so you won't receive all of the interest in one year. If you don't want to pay taxes on the accrued interest, exchange the bonds for the HH series.

# CHAPTER 15

# Protecting your estate without hurting your retirement

EVERY NOW AND THEN, YOU'LL READ ABOUT SOMEONE WHO LIVED MODestly for years in a shabby house and drove an old car, yet left millions to relatives or a charity. The person lived simply and accumulated a great deal of money. The vast majority of people, however, want to enjoy the fruits of their labor.

Many people want to protect their retirement and still leave money for their heirs. Others want to spend every dime and never cut themselves short on cash. Estate planning is important for either type of person, especially if you have a spouse or partner who probably isn't going to die on the same day you do. And no matter how well-planned your retirement is, it may end before you expected.

If you're like most people, your goal is to live life to its fullest and to leave a legacy for your loved ones or a charity. To achieve that goal, you may need a good lawyer to guide you and the right legal documents to assure that your wishes are respected in life or death.

## BACK TO BASICS

Estate planning is much more than writing a will to distribute your property after you die. Estate planning is the process used to shelter your assets from taxes and to ensure that your property is distributed to your heirs in the most efficient manner. Estate planning also enables you to provide for the management of your affairs if you become incapacitated. It also ensures that your instructions will be carried out if you're unable to do so yourself.

You don't need to be wealthy to have an estate plan. Almost anyone can benefit from estate planning.

Despite what you may have heard about the estate tax being abolished, it's still here now and may be around for years to come. The basic exclusion from federal estate taxes is $1 million in 2003. Unless the law is changed again, the estate tax will disappear entirely in 2010 but will reappear once more in 2011. You also have state death taxes to consider.

Probate is the act of authenticating your will and making sure that assets are properly distributed to your heirs. If your estate is complicated, it can be a costly and time-consuming affair. Many assets, such as life insurance, avoid the probate process and go directly to the beneficiary named on the document. Bank accounts also avoid the probate process, because they normally transfer at death to the co-owner or the beneficiaries named in the banking documents.

Even if property is transferred directly to a co-owner or a beneficiary, it will normally be included in the taxable estate. For example, if you own a $500,000 life insurance policy that names your children as beneficiaries, they'll receive the proceeds without going through the probate process. Nevertheless, that $500,000 is part of your taxable estate and may be subject to estate taxes.

## FINDING A GOOD LAWYER TO HELP WITH
## ESTATE PLANNING

In the "Dilbert" comic strip, Dilbert is in a lawyer's office for advice about estate planning. Upon hearing that he can avoid probate costs by creating a living trust, Dilbert says, "So . . . I can use an inconvenient system created by lawyers to avoid a worse system created by lawyers." The attorney responds by saying, "According to my watch, that witty observation cost you four dollars."

When you're in a lawyer's office, you may feel the meter is running from the moment you sit down. You may, however, need good legal advice to protect your estate. You're probably aware that estate planning is more than just writing a will. And for most people, you need more than a do-it-yourself estate plan.

Most people don't know how to find a lawyer, let alone one who can help with estate planning. A study for Lawyers.com by Yankelovich in Chapel Hill, North Carolina, found that less than 30 percent of people surveyed knew where to start looking for an attorney. A lawyer who advertises on television or in the Yellow Pages isn't necessarily the right attorney to handle your estate planning issues.

The quest for the best attorney to help protect your estate is easier in some states. In those states, the bar association conducts a certification program for legal specialties like estate planning. If an attorney is certified in estate planning or a related field, you'll know that he specializes in that area and possesses certain qualifications that other lawyers might not have. Although any lawyer can draft a simple will, estate planning is much more complicated and may require someone with significant expertise and experience.

Ask friends, relatives, and business associates for recommendations. Make sure they used the lawyer for estate planning and not an unrelated matter like criminal law. Naturally, you'll want to be sure they were happy with the lawyer's demeanor and fees, and with the results. You should also check with your county's bar association to see if it offers a lawyer referral service.

Another source of information is a national directory of lawyers published by Martindale-Hubbell. It contains biographical information about attorneys in every state. This multivolume set is available in most public libraries, as well as online at www.martindale.com.

Check to see if your state has online access to any disciplinary action that might have been taken against the attorney. If not, the lawyer disciplinary board in your state or the bar association might keep public records on attorneys whose clients have complained.

Once you've found some good candidates, call and ask for an estimate of the fees and whether there is a charge for an initial consultation. The written fee agreement should spell out the charges.

## WHAT LEGAL DOCUMENTS DO YOU NEED?

An elderly man in Sunrise, Florida, died believing he had all the legal documents his family needed to quickly and painlessly settle his estate. He had a living trust that would transfer ownership of his property to his son and daughter. The man didn't know that the living trust was missing some important language. As a result, his only asset, a $38,000 condominium, couldn't be sold for months because of the defective living trust. Consequently, it cost his family thousands of dollars in legal fees to resolve the dilemma.

In this gentleman's case, the problematic living trust did not live up to its billing as an effective way to transfer property and avoid the probate process. The document was drafted poorly and caused headaches for the family. Despite this family's bad experience, however, estate planning usually pays off.

There are many legal documents you need, but hope you'll never need. You also need a competent attorney to draft them, because homemade legal forms can open a can of worms. No matter what your age, you need a valid will. Living trusts are pitched at seminars in retirement areas across the country, but they are no substitute for a will. Even if the living trust is properly drafted, you still need a will to dispose of any remaining property.

A durable power of attorney allows a family member or trusted friend to manage your assets if you're incapable of managing them yourself. The durable power of attorney is a legal document that authorizes someone to act as the agent or attorney-in-fact for another person. This authority continues, even if the person becomes incapacitated or incompetent. Watch out, however, because giving a durable power of attorney to an untrustworthy individual can cost you dearly.

Depending on the legal requirements in your state, you may need a healthcare proxy or a durable power of attorney for healthcare. You designate a family member or trusted friend to make medical decisions for you if you're incapacitated and can't make those decisions yourself.

A living will is not the same as a will that distributes property after your death. The living will contains instructions regarding what type of medical care you want if you're incapable of making your wishes known. These instructions might also be referred to as advanced directives for healthcare.

Despite the experience of the man in Sunrise, Florida, you might need a trust agreement of some kind. For example, the revocable living trust, if prepared correctly, helps your estate avoid probate. Nevertheless, because the trust is revocable, the assets remain in the taxable estate. An irrevocable living trust is needed to remove assets from the taxable estate.

There are also trusts that can provide for a child with special needs or your favorite charity. Some charitable gifts can even provide a source of income. The charitable gift annuity provides an immediate tax deduction based on the amount you give to charity and your age. The charitable gift annuity also pays you a specified amount each year. An accountant, lawyer, financial planner, or the gift planning office of the charity can outline some of your options.

## PROTECTION TIPS

Estate planning goes hand in hand with creating a blueprint for retirement. In both situations, you're taking an inventory of your assets and liabilities. You're ascertaining the current value of your investments, as well as any personal property you own. In addition, you're taking stock of any benefits you get through work, such as a retirement plan or insurance. As you build assets to finance your retirement or withdraw funds from your nest egg, you must also decide how you want your property disposed of during your lifetime or at the time of your death.

You may be a candidate for estate planning, even if you don't think your estate is large. Many people with average incomes build a large estate, thanks to a growing 401(k) or a house that has skyrocketed in value. As you examine your financial situation in preparation for retirement, you should also determine the size of your estate and how you want it to be distributed.

Even though legal forms are available in books and on the Internet, you really need customized documents prepared by a competent attorney. Every adult should have a will and a living will, even if you'd rather not think about death and dying.

Much as you may think that any attorney can help to protect your estate, you really need someone who specializes in these matters. Even if your estate isn't complicated, a lawyer in general practice may not have sufficient expertise to properly advise you.

# CHAPTER 16

# Protecting your retirement
# from fraud

In an ad for a financial services firm, a slimy manager is urging his salespeople to push an overpriced security. The salespeople are working in what appears to be a "boiler room," which is a temporary office filled with phones where salespeople call lists of prospects with the hope of selling them worthless or overpriced securities. The manager promises game tickets to the salesperson duping the most customers into buying the stock. His final words to the group are, "OK, people. Let's put some lipstick on this pig."

An unethical, smooth-talking salesperson can make the worst investment look good. An estimated $10 billion per year is lost due to fraud against consumers. And that figure doesn't include fraud by corporate executives who cook the books to mislead investors.

Investors usually get themselves in trouble when they look for nontraditional investments from financial advisers they don't know or shouldn't trust. When interest rates are low and stock prices are down, investors are quicker to believe a sales pitch that promises a great return on their investment. You also have more individuals who are willing to act unethically or commit fraud to make a living.

You don't need to be an ultraconservative investor to protect your retirement. Nevertheless, you do need to avoid investments that have a serious potential for fraud, as well as salespeople and financial services professionals who aren't looking out for your best interests.

## PROTECTING YOURSELF FROM SCAMS

Protecting your retirement from fraud gets a little tougher as you age. You might not be as sharp as you once were. On the other hand, you should be a better judge of people. No matter how old you are, it's important to have people looking out for your best interests, whether it's a trusted friend or relative, a financial planner, a lawyer, an accountant, or all of them as a form of checks and balances. If you're at all concerned about a particular person or transaction, contact state and local regulators for guidance.

The old rules of thumb haven't changed. If an investment sounds too good to be true, it probably is. Don't let greed get the best of you. When interest rates are 2 percent and stocks are in the tank, ask yourself how someone can guarantee a profit of 15 percent to 20 percent.

Each year, the North American Securities Administrators Administration (NASAA) releases a list of the top ten investment scams, risky investments, or sales practices being investigated by state securities regulators. New to the list released on August 26, 2002, were unscrupulous brokers, conflict of interest problems with research analysts, fraudulent oil and gas investments, and schemes involving charitable gift annuities. This doesn't mean that all charitable gift annuities, or oil and gas investments, are scams. It just means that state securities regulators ran into people who were exploiting them for their own gain.

**THE TOP TEN INVESTMENT SCAMS INVESTIGATED BY STATE SECURITIES REGULATORS**

1. Unlicensed individuals, such as independent insurance agents, selling fraudulent or risky securities
2. Unscrupulous stockbrokers
3. Analyst research conflicts
4. Promissory notes
5. "Prime bank" schemes
6. Viatical settlements
7. Affinity fraud
8. Charitable gift annuities
9. Oil and gas schemes
10. Equipment leasing

Source: North American Securities Administrators Administration, www.nasaa.org

## BE CAREFUL OUT THERE

On the classic cop series *Hill Street Blues*, Sergeant Phil Esterhaus warned officers to be careful out there. To protect your retirement, you also need to be careful out there.

Oil and gas scams are quite common. You might run into unlicensed stock brokers who are selling phony shares of natural gas companies and oil exploration firms.

As mentioned in Chapter 15, charitable gift annuities are offered by many legitimate charitable organizations. You donate a large amount to the charity in cash or property. In return, you receive a charitable deduction for a portion of the amount donated and an income stream for life or some specified term. The problem arises, however, with phony charities that serve no legitimate charitable purpose and do not have the assets to make good on the annuity.

Similarly, affinity fraud involves scam artists who use their victim's religious or ethnic identity to build trust. The scam artists then wring donations from their victims and steal their savings. They might also pitch inappropriate investments to people who have let their guard down.

Most investors should refrain from investing in promissory notes. Start-up companies often use promissory notes to finance their short-term borrowing needs. Typically, the investor lends the money, thinking the loan is bonded by an insurance company. If the start-up company fails, however, the investor may find out the insurance company isn't legitimate.

Sometimes, the promissory notes are issued by nonexistent companies. They promise high returns and little risk. In Georgia, scam artists recruited independent insurance agents to sells millions of dollars worth of promissory notes. Half of the money taken in was paid as commissions to salespeople and the people behind the scam.

Certain investments aren't appropriate for people interested in protecting their retirement. Investing in commodities isn't a good strategy for unsophisticated investors. Penny stocks are also too risky for most investors.

The United States Postal Service has also issued warnings about illegal telemarketing and mail fraud schemes aimed at consumers. You can find out more at www.usps.com/postalinspectors.

There are also thousands of useless products sold each year. The September 2002 *AARP Bulletin* (www.aarp.org.bulletin/scamalert) reported that consumers were sold a $1,200 magnetic mattress pad that promised relief from high cholesterol, diabetes, Alzheimer's disease, heart disease, and other ailments. If you're even thinking about buying products like these, and you shouldn't be, contact the Federal Trade Commission (FTC) first or your state attorney general's office. The telephone number for the FTC is 1-877-987-3728.

## VIATICALS

Viaticals sound at first like a win-win situation for all the parties, but you may be the big loser. Viatical settlements are lump sum payments to

individuals who are terminally ill in exchange for the death benefit of their life insurance policy. A viatical settlement allows the terminally ill insured to collect on her life insurance policy prior to death. The person who receives the money can use it to enjoy those final days. The insured receives a percentage of the face value of the policy that is based on life expectancy.

In its simplest form, an investor provides the cash used for that viatical settlement. When the insured dies, investors receive the return on their investment. Even if you can get past the ghoulish nature of viatical settlements, there are serious risks for the investor. The insured may live much longer than expected, which delays the investor's profits. Furthermore, the insured might not be nearly as sick as the investor is led to believe and might be undergoing life-saving treatment. In addition, if the viatical company goes under, investors may lose some or all of their investments.

## DECEPTIVE SALES TACTICS

While most financial services professionals are decent human beings who want to help their clients, there have been many allegations of deceptive sales practices in recent years. Deceptive sales tactics can undermine your retirement. To protect your retirement, you need to keep your guard up.

When you hear terms like the shell game, Ponzi schemes, bait-and-switch, and other colorful phrases, you automatically think of scams. In the financial services arena, the unethical sales tactics go by names like churning, twisting, and sliding. Although these sales practices can lead to sanctions by insurance and securities regulators, many go undetected.

### Life insurance sold as a retirement plan

Deceptive sales tactics have led to many suits against financial services companies. One large insurance company sold life insurance under the pretense that it was a retirement plan. Agents did their best to hide all

references to life insurance in the marketing materials. The consumers were told they were buying an investment, not life insurance.

Although life insurance certainly plays a major role in financial planning for retirement, it may constitute a deceptive sales practice to go too far. Misrepresenting whole life insurance as a retirement plan is a deceptive sales method. Agents may not deliberately obscure the fact that they're selling life insurance by calling it a retirement plan.

## Vanishing premiums that never vanish

When insurance agents tell customers that their premiums will vanish, they are saying that dividends will exceed the amount of the premiums owed and there will be no out-of-pocket cost to the policyholder. One problem with these statements is that dividends are never guaranteed by the insurance company. If dividends are reduced, the consumer finds out that the policy is not "paid up" as the agent said in his sales pitch.

In most cases, the salesperson assures the customer that by making larger payments at the beginning, the policy will become self-sufficient. According to the agent, there will be enough money in the accumulation fund to cover future mortality charges and administrative costs. But if interest rates plunge, there may not be enough to cover the cost of the policy. The customer still has to pay premiums or lose the policy.

Policies with so-called abbreviated payment schedules can cause problems much like vanishing premium cases. Customers are told that after a number of years, accumulated dividends will cover the premiums, and they will not owe any more money. However, that only works if the dividend rate stays the same or increases. If the dividend drops, the customer will continue getting bills.

## Sliding

One needs to watch out for tactics such as misrepresentation, over-insuring, and sliding. Like a magician doing a card trick, an unethical salesperson may slide forms in front of customers without providing a complete or truthful explanation of what they're signing and buying. Customers rely on the salesperson's explanation and don't read the documents. The victim of sliding may sign away certain rights without realizing it.

## Churning and twisting

The terms "churning" and "twisting" don't refer to a new dance, but are deceptive sales practices. Churning is more common in the securities industry. For example, a stockbroker is constantly buying and selling stocks for an elderly retiree. He does this strictly to rake in commissions, not because anything has changed about those particular investments.

Churning is now associated with insurance sales as well. It is the practice whereby the assets (cash value, loan values, dividends) in an existing life insurance policy or annuity contract are utilized to purchase another insurance policy or annuity contract with that same insurer for the purpose of earning additional premiums, fees, commissions, or other compensation. The unethical insurance salesperson pushes a customer to replace one perfectly good policy with another. Several life insurance companies and agents have admitted that they talked customers into giving up one policy to buy another. This helped the company sell larger policies and gave the agent another sizable commission.

Churning has taken place if any of the following occur:

- The salesperson has no reasonable basis for believing that the replacement will result in an actual and demonstrable benefit to the policyholder.
- The sale takes place in a fashion that is fraudulent, deceptive, or misleading, or involves a deceptive omission.
- The customer is not informed that the existing policy cash values, dividends, or other assets will be reduced, forfeited, or utilized to purchase the replacement or additional policy.
- The customer is not informed that the replacement or additional policy isn't paid up or that more premiums may be owed at some point.

Twisting encompasses any of the following acts for the purpose of inducing a person to lapse, forfeit, surrender, terminate, or borrow on any policy in order to take out a policy from another insurer:

- To knowingly make any misleading representations
- To knowingly make any incomplete or fraudulent comparisons
- To knowingly make any fraudulent material omissions

These improper acts can relate to the old or new policy or the insurer.

With cash-value life insurance products, most of the administrative and selling costs are applied to the premiums in the early years. When consumers trade in one policy for another, they pay those costs a second time.

There are additional risks when one policy is traded in for another. In every life insurance policy, there is an incontestability period, which is typically two years. After two years, the insurer may usually not challenge any claims presented. When an old policy is traded in for a new one, the incontestability period begins again, and the insurance company may contest any claim that might arise during that two-year time frame.

State insurance regulations pertaining to replacement do not outlaw replacement of one policy with another. They do, however, put certain safeguards in place to make certain the replacement is justified. Even if the replacement is justified, the salesperson and the insurance company will be penalized if the appropriate disclosures are not given to the customer.

## PEOPLE WHO CAN HELP PROTECT YOUR RETIREMENT FROM FRAUD

You're not alone in your battle to protect your retirement from fraud. There are people you can hire, as well as government agencies that will stand behind you.

Every family needs a lawyer it can turn to for legal advice. Hopefully, it's someone you trust implicitly. We talked earlier about lawyers who specialize in estate planning, but there may be other occasions where you need to hire a competent and caring attorney. When you buy a new home to live in during retirement or a vacation home, you'll probably need a competent real estate attorney to look over the paperwork.

Even if your tax situation isn't too complicated, you may need to engage the services of a tax professional. As we saw in Chapter 14, the tax laws relating to retirement accounts are quite complicated, and a mistake can cost you far more than you'll pay to an accountant.

An ethical insurance agent can make life easier for you in retirement. As you approach retirement, you're at the age when you should be considering long-term care insurance. The agent can also help you find health insurance and Medigap policies if you need them. As mentioned above, be wary of any agent who wants to sell you policies to replace ones you already have. Be careful also, because an insurance agent is not the right person to give general financial planning advice. Many agents will only recommend insurance products to protect and rebuild your retirement, even though many other investments are more suitable.

## CHOOSING A FINANCIAL ADVISER

In a "Dilbert" cartoon, a full-service stockbroker, Bob Weaselton, introduces himself to Dilbert. Weaselton says, "I can act as if brokers know which stocks are better than others. Then I'll earn your trust by comparing your portfolio to misleading benchmarks." Weaselton then offers Dilbert another option. "I sell you whatever garbage earns me the biggest commission," he says.

Hopefully, you'll find a more ethical financial adviser than Dilbert did. A financial adviser can offer specific advice on protecting your retirement. Ideally, the adviser will have no vested interest in the investments that she recommends.

To find the right financial adviser, ask friends, relatives, and business associates for recommendations. Don't pick someone just because you see an advertisement in the newspaper. Furthermore, just because someone is on the radio or television, or gives you a free lunch at an all-you-can-eat buffet, is no assurance that the individual is competent and ethical. Often, these financial mavens buy time from the radio or television station, and the entire program is just an infomercial.

Look for educational credentials like the Certified Financial Planner (CFP) designation. The CFP designation means the adviser has extensive training and abides by a strict ethical code. The Certified Financial Planner must meet certain educational standards, possess three years or more of financial planning experience, and pass a two-day exam covering subjects like insurance, investments, taxes, and estate planning. You can check on a financial planner's certification by calling 1-888-237-6275.

The Financial Planning Association lists CFPs across the country on its website (www.fpanet.org/plannersearch). You can also call 800-647-6340 for a referral. If your situation is unusual and extremely complicated, you can find CFPs who specialize in some particular aspect of financial planning. Most CFPs, however, are generalists and can help clients with almost any kind of financial planning issue.

Although CFPs have tax expertise, another possibility is to talk with a Certified Public Accountant (CPA). There are CPAs who also give financial planning advice. These CPAs hold the Personal Financial Specialist (PFS) designation. More information is available on the Internet at www.cpapfs.org or by calling 888-999-9256.

## How financial advisers are compensated

Always ask how the planner is compensated for financial planning advice. The financial adviser should not be offended when you ask how he is compensated. Generally, you'll pay a flat fee or an hourly charge for unbiased financial planning advice. Some financial advisers may charge a percentage of the assets they manage for you, often 1 percent every year. Planners who belong to the National Association of Personal Financial Advisors (www.napfa.org) operate on a fee-only basis and charge hourly rates of anywhere from $50 to $300.

Even if a financial adviser charges a set fee, she may make a commission on the products recommended. Some financial advisers charge no fee, but earn a commission on the products recommended. This gives the adviser an incentive to recommend certain products and places limits on solutions. If the planner only sells insurance, it's a good bet that the solution will involve your buying an insurance product.

## Red flags when dealing with financial advisers

The adviser should only be recommending investments that are suitable for someone with your investment temperament. If you lose sleep when a stock you own goes down a point, the market isn't for you. Your financial adviser should explain the potential upside and downside of every investment recommended. If all you're hearing is the upside, this is probably not the right financial adviser for you.

You should always deal with someone who knows when additional expertise is needed. A good financial planner knows when to call in a lawyer or accountant.

As we've seen throughout this book, your retirement can be jeopardized, even when people are genuinely looking out for your well-being. Sadly, there are many people out there who don't have your best interests at heart.

### CHECKING OUT INVESTMENT ADVISERS AND BROKERS

Investment advisers must register with the Securities and Exchange Commission (SEC) if they manage $25 million or more in client assets. If the adviser manages less than $25 million, registration is required with the state securities agency in the state where she has a principal place of business.

You can check out an investment adviser's background at the SEC's Investment Adviser Public Disclosure website (www .adviserinfo.sec.gov). You'll be able to review the adviser's ADV. The ADV is a full disclosure form on which you can find information about the adviser's educational background, as well as any problems the individual has had with regulators and clients. Part two of the ADV form outlines the adviser's services, fees, and strategies.

Make sure you have the adviser's Central Registration Depository (CRD) number. The CRD is a computerized database that contains information regarding most advisers and the firms for which they work. You can find out if the adviser is licensed in your state and whether there have been complaints against that person. The CRD number should be on the adviser's ADV.

Before dealing with any broker or financial professional, place a call to the National Association of Securities Dealers (NASD) at 1-800-289-9999 and check on the individual's disciplinary record. The website is www.nasd.com. You can also investigate a financial adviser by contacting the state agency that regulates securities. These regulators are listed on the North American Securities Administrators Association, Inc.'s website, which can be found at www.nasaa.org. Your state's insurance department may also have licensing and complaint information regarding certain financial advisers.

## PROTECTION TIPS

Fraud can destroy your blueprint for retirement. If you're a victim, you can be left without a plan and may be forced to start rebuilding your retirement at the age you expected to retire.

No matter who is recommending the investment, do your own research. If you're not comfortable with the Internet, ask a friend or relative for help in doing the research.

There are many ways to reduce your chances of being victimized. The first is to avoid cold calls from people you don't know, claiming to offer a great investment product. Don't even consider an investment opportunity unless you're dealing with a financial professional who's licensed and in good standing with state regulators. The person should also come highly recommended from people you know and trust. Nevertheless, it's always possible that they're being victimized too.

If you don't understand the investment, stay away from it. If an investment sounds too good to be true, it probably is. You always have to wonder why the people promoting these incredible investment opportunities need to share them with you instead of getting rich themselves.

Write down your investment goals and don't stray from them. If you're seeking modest growth and little risk, stick with investment products that are consistent with those goals.

If you're knowingly taking a risk with your money, make sure it's an amount you can afford to lose. Get-rich-quick schemes are usually just that, schemes. You're not protecting your retirement; you're putting it at risk.

Before making a commitment, look to your attorney, accountant, or financial adviser for guidance. Don't allow yourself to be pressured into making a decision on the spot. If you have been pressured into signing, seek help immediately from a lawyer or the state regulators who monitor these products.

It is a deceptive sales practice for an insurance agent to lie about the extent of coverage or to talk customers into policies they don't need. Deceptive sales practices may be used to sell any kind of a policy, whether it's auto, homeowners, disability, health, life, or long-term care insurance.

Deceptive sales practices are more than just the hard sell. Nevertheless, high-pressure sales tactics are frowned upon by insurance regulators. Most states give insurance buyers thirty days to cancel a policy, so they'll have time to reconsider a purchase from an overly aggressive agent.

Most states have "do not call" laws protecting consumers from unwanted telemarketers. Contact the appropriate state office, usually the attorney general, to get on the do not call list. Even if there's no law in your state, demand that the telemarketer put you on its internal do not call list.

# CHAPTER 17

# Working to protect and
# enhance your retirement

You may picture yourself living out your retirement in a sleepy little town, miles from nowhere, where there's nothing to do but fish. Unfortunately, however, you may need to reconsider that lifestyle if the only job available is in a bait shop and some other retiree already has that position nailed down.

Some people don't seem to understand that it's possible to retire and still work. In their minds, you're either retired or you're working. In reality, retirement doesn't necessarily mean that you'll never hold a job again. You may decide to explore a new career or open a business. One way of looking at the situation is that you've retired from one career to pursue another. It's not uncommon for a new line of work to go hand-in-hand with retirement.

Because of the bear market, many readers will postpone their original retirement date and continue working. As we've seen throughout this book, there are other options such as cutting your spending and scaling back on your plans for retirement. Staying at a job you love to protect your retirement may be the right choice for you. It's more difficult to justify that choice, however, if you've grown to hate what you're doing for a living.

In a bookstore in Boca Raton, Florida, a man was complaining about his career to a group of friends. The man, who appeared to be in his sixties, was telling the group that he had worked for his former employer for thirty-six years. He hated the company and he hated the people. After retiring, the man then went back to work for the same company as a consultant for five more years and hated every minute of the experience.

Protecting your retirement shouldn't mean working at a job that you say you hate. Ideally, you'll find work that enriches your life, even if it doesn't make you rich. The extra money should keep you from depleting your nest egg and shouldn't reduce your Social Security check. Hopefully, that job will give you a feeling of financial freedom, rather than making you feel locked in.

## WORKING OUT OF NECESSITY, NOT CHOICE

In the sports world, it's not uncommon to hear about people "unretiring." Hockey player Mario Lemieux and Michael Jordan came out of retirement. The big difference is that they unretired out of choice, not necessity. That distinction makes a world of difference. Their situation is much different than that of a destitute boxer who keeps coming out of retirement for one more fight and risks permanent brain damage or worse.

In the real world, people are often forced to unretire out of necessity, not choice. Depending upon your situation, you might need extra money to pay for prescriptions or for luxury items like dinners at fancy restaurants or a special trip.

Receiving a paycheck, even a small one, means you'll draw less money from your nest egg. That income means you'll have more ready cash, so you can avoid cashing in some of your investments when they are down in value.

An AARP study, "Beyond Fifty: A Report to the Nation on Economic Security," has found that retirement does not necessarily mean terminating employment. Many preretirees, who are defined as age 52 to age 61, as well as younger retirees (age 62 to age 74), view retirement as a time for transition, not the end of work. The income they earn from working helps to secure their retirement.

A more recent AARP survey, conducted by Roper ASW, interviewed workers age 45 to age 74. Seventy-six percent said the fact that they enjoy the job or enjoy working is a major factor in why they keep working. Seventy-six percent also said they keep working because they need the money. Sixty-nine percent said they plan to work in retirement. A Harris Interactive survey for AIG SunAmerica reported that 95 percent of pre-retirees expect to work in some capacity after they retire.

In addition to these surveys, there are scientific studies showing that inactivity is a huge threat to physical and mental health. Work can provide social opportunities and a chance to interact with people. You can keep your mind active, and it's less likely you'll be bored.

Although inactivity is a threat to your physical and mental health, certain jobs can be dangerous. In Spokane, Washington, a woman wrote to an advice columnist regarding the risks of delivering newspapers in the winter. The woman related that she and her husband are part of a growing number of people in their fifties and sixties who supplement their fixed incomes by delivering newspapers door-to-door. Although she enjoys the extra money and the exercise, the woman expressed concern that they might fall on icy or snowy steps in the wee hours of the morning.

Protecting and rebuilding your retirement might require you to work full-time or part-time, or to unretire at some point. Even if you're working out of necessity, not choice, you'll hopefully enjoy what you're doing and won't risk breaking a hip on icy steps. It's also important that you not feel trapped in a particular job. The ideal situation is knowing that you can call it quits at the end of the day if the job is too stressful or you aren't enjoying the work.

You shouldn't feel locked in to one particular job at one particular company. There are no guarantees that the job will last forever or even until next month. It would be a shame if the job keeps you up nights, either due to aggravation or fear that the company will be closing its doors.

## THE IMPACT OF WORK ON WHERE YOU WANT TO LIVE

If you plan to golf every day in retirement, you wouldn't move to an area where there are few if any golf courses. Similarly, if you plan to work full- or part-time during retirement, you shouldn't move to an area where there are few if any job opportunities. Even if your age is not a barrier to landing a job, the location you choose may limit your options for finding meaningful work.

As you decide where you want to live in retirement, you need to look at the work opportunities that are available in that community. Even if you don't expect to work in retirement, think about what employment opportunities exist in the place you're considering. Tied in with this decision is the question of what you want to do with your time. If you're considering a new career in a different field, make sure you can pursue those interests in the place you're considering for retirement.

Try to avoid logistical problems for yourself. A couple moving from New York to Florida wanted to work, but they were betwixt and between. They were reluctant to find a job in New York, because they planned to move as soon as their house sold. The couple wasn't ready to find work in Florida, because they didn't want to move until their new home was ready.

Ideally, you can make some money wherever you decide to live. If you have certain skills, all you'll need is a computer, and you can work from your house, whether it's where you're living now or next to the bait shop in some sleepy town.

## DIFFERENT APPROACHES TO
## WORKING IN RETIREMENT

In October 2002, John Fenn, age 85, and two other scientists were awarded the Nobel Prize in Chemistry. Fenn's research helped to inspire a revolution in biomedical research. According to *The Washington Post*, Fenn maintains a full work schedule in his own laboratory in Richmond, Virginia.

Many people will argue that work is an important component in our lives, no matter how old we get to be. Many older Americans never adjust to retirement. They really have no interests other than work. Others, however, are champing at the bit to retire and adjust beautifully to retirement. They have dozens of interests they want to pursue.

Part-time work is ideal for many. It keeps your mind active. You stay involved with people and have a wonderful balance between work and play. There is still ample time to pursue other interests.

A report from the Employee Benefit Research Institute (EBRI) found that many older Americans leave the workforce gradually and find bridge jobs. Bridge jobs are part-time or short-term positions, either in your chosen line of work or a totally new field. In some cases, the bridge job involves a shift to self-employment.

EBRI's study found that one-third to one-half of older workers will hold a bridge job before they drop out of the workforce completely. Workers take on these bridge jobs so they can remain economically active and sometimes to bring in needed income.

We looked in Chapter 11 at the concept of phased retirement. A bridge job might be part of a phased retirement program, or you might be working for a new employer in a totally different industry. The danger with phased retirement, however, is that it may have a negative effect on your pension and Social Security, because you'll be earning much less in your final years of employment.

Unless you've reached the full retirement age, working can have a detrimental impact on your Social Security check. As we saw in Chapter 10, you lose one dollar in Social Security benefits for each two dollars you earn that exceeds the earnings threshold. In 2003, the earnings threshold is $11,520.

Jumping back into the workforce isn't easy. Adam Geller of the Associated Press wrote about Bob Blakeslee of Springfield, Massachusetts. When his investments soured, Blakeslee was forced back into the workforce. Although Blakeslee once earned more than $100,000 per year designing corporate retirement plans, the only job he can find now pays

$7.50 per hour. His son, who is a sophomore in high school, makes $8 per hour as a dishwasher in a restaurant.

You hear and read a lot about how businesses are desperately in need of older workers with skills and experience that younger workers don't have. While there may be certain fields in which older workers are in demand, you might not find employers breaking down doors to hire you. Many experts believe age discrimination is a reality, and older workers may have difficulty finding meaningful employment. According to the Equal Employment Opportunity Commission, age discrimination claims jumped 40 percent from 1999 to 2002.

You may not realize how tough it is to find a job in certain areas of the country and in certain fields. You might even find it demeaning to look for work. The last time you looked for work may have been in the 1960s or 1970s.

## Opening Your Own Business

Some retirees dream of opening their own business. This is a risky proposition, especially if you use some of your retirement nest egg to buy a franchise or for start-up expenses. Don't underestimate how demanding and expensive it can be to open up your own business. Chances are, you'll work harder than you ever did.

Operating a small business does have advantages. You can keep contributing to special retirement accounts for small businesses. You may be able to deduct trips that combine business and pleasure. In addition, you also may be able to deduct the cost of health insurance. In 2003, the self-employed may be able to deduct 100 percent of their health insurance premiums.

Many people dream of turning a hobby into a business after they finish their traditional career. A good time to start your business is before you retire. By doing so, you'll find out if your hobby has the makings of a profitable business and whether you enjoy it as much when your goal is making money. If you do make money, you can contribute a percentage of the profit to a SEP (simplified employee pension) or another retirement account for small businesses.

## PROTECTION TIPS

As you develop your blueprint to protect and rebuild your retirement, you should plan on working. Write down the types of jobs you would enjoy working at on a part-time or temporary basis. Also, jot down what industries appeal to you, even if no particular job comes to mind. Make a list of your parameters, such as salary, hours, and time off.

Ideally, if you need to work to protect your retirement, you won't subject yourself to the same stress you face now. Hopefully, you'll find a position that gives meaning to your life or keeps you vibrant.

Don't underestimate how tough job-hunting is on your ego and self-esteem. If you've held management positions for many years, it's difficult to go back to being the low man or woman on the totem pole. You might find yourself working for someone who is thirty years or more younger than you.

Opening a business in a field you know nothing about isn't the solution to protecting your retirement. You might drain your nest egg to fund the business. The new business may turn out to be a money pit that eats up all of your savings and destroys the financial foundation of your retirement.

# CHAPTER 18

# Protecting your portfolio

COMEDIAN GROUCHO MARX LOST A FORTUNE DURING THE STOCK MARKET crash of 1929. Marx joked, however, that he was lucky: "I would have lost more, but that was all the money I had." It's hard to laugh, however, as you watch years of savings disappear during a stock market crash or a sustained bear market.

In October 2002, Sir John Templeton, one of the world's most respected financial experts, confessed to Louis Rukeyser that he had no idea when the bear market would end. If the experts like Templeton are stumped, where does that leave the rest of us?

Other experts made bold predictions that didn't come true. Betsy Stark aired a report for ABC News called "False Prophets." Stark reported that investment strategist Abby Joseph Cohen predicted that the Dow Jones Industrial Average would finish at 11,300 in 2002. In October of 2002, Cohen revised her prediction and wrote that the Dow would finish

at 10,800. Unfortunately for Cohen and investors, the Dow closed the
year at 8,341.63.

Predicting the fortunes of individual stocks isn't easy either. According to Stark in the same news report, legendary investor George Soros
bought 2 million shares of United Airlines stock in 2002. The airline
later filed for bankruptcy protection in December 2002. Although he is
reportedly worth about $7 billion, Soros had a tough year. He was con-
victed of insider trading in France.

## STRATEGIES TO PROTECT YOUR PORTFOLIO

There will be times when there's nowhere to hide in the stock market.
U.S. stock mutual funds lost 22 percent in 2002. This decline in value
was larger than stock fund declines in 2001 and 2000. Despite those
losses, you still need stocks to protect and rebuild your portfolio.

As was stressed before, the asset allocation strategy pushes you to
invest in other asset classes. If you ignore asset allocation and rebalancing,
you probably sat through the latest bear market with all of your money in
stock funds. During that time frame, your pain would have been eased by
the performance of the bond market. According to Lehman Brothers Inc.,
the total return for bond investors in 2002 was 10.2 percent. During 2000
through 2002, bonds performed better than stocks.

Judging by history, that will change in years to come, especially if
interest rates rise dramatically and bond prices fall. According to Ibbotson
Associates, the average annual return for stocks from 1926 to 2001 was
10.7 percent. The average annual return for bonds from 1926 to 2001
was 5.3 percent. Even as stocks recover and the bond market falters, you
need to stick with the asset allocation strategy.

### Dollar cost averaging and averaging down

When you're rebuilding your stock portfolio, dollar cost averaging is still
the best long-term strategy, as long as you know its limitations. It works
best with low-cost mutual funds that utilize different styles of investing.

With dollar cost averaging, you know the average price you pay for each share will usually be favorable.

Dollar cost averaging doesn't work when you're only investing in a few individual stocks. For example, in 1999, Lucent sold for eight-four dollars per share. In October 2002, shares were selling for fifty-eight cents. If Lucent were one of only two or three stocks in your portfolio, the dollar cost averaging strategy wouldn't have worked. The strategy is also undermined if you invest in a mutual fund that charges a sales fee every time you invest.

The averaging down strategy resembles dollar cost averaging, but it can be extremely dangerous. To average down means to purchase additional stock in a company you already own when the shares drop in price from your earlier purchase. During a bear market, you'll see stocks hitting new lows, and some financial advisers will tell clients to average down by buying more shares as the price goes lower.

With that advice, you might keep buying more shares of a stock that's never going to recover. Even if you're not in a bear market, there may be good reasons why a stock is going lower. You might want to think about selling the shares you already own, not buying more.

You can also average down when you're investing in mutual funds. You might decide to invest more if shares fall in value. By doing so, you're trying to outguess the market, instead of taking a systematic approach to investing. The mutual fund shares may go down and stay down.

## EXCHANGE TRADED FUNDS

Exchange traded funds can give you a great deal of diversity. Each share of an exchange traded fund represents a basket of securities. Although they resemble mutual funds, exchange traded funds are bought and sold like stocks. Because they are not actively managed, exchange traded funds offer expense ratios that may be even lower than index funds. Expense ratios average roughly 0.2 of 1 percent.

There are more than one hundred exchange traded funds listed on the American Stock Exchange (www.amex.com). A very popular exchange traded fund is the SPDR, which stands for Standard & Poor's Depository Receipt, or Spider. They are advertised as providing instant diversification. Spiders track the value of an index such as the S&P 500, which consists of large company stocks. There are also Spiders that track the S&P MidCap 400 stocks, as well as other indexes.

There are many exchange traded funds from which to choose. For example, you can purchase iShares, which trade on the American Stock Exchange, the Chicago Board of Options Exchange, and the New York Stock Exchange. You can buy and sell them through any brokerage account. When you buy iShares, you're purchasing shares of a portfolio that tracks the performance of a particular market index. Like an index fund, you own a pool of securities. With a single trade, you can buy or sell the portfolio contained in each share.

When you buy iShares, you get diversification with very low expenses. You can easily combine the growth and value approaches to investing in the stock market. For example, you can buy the iShares Russell 1000 Value Index. Those shares seek investment results that correspond to the performance of U.S. large-cap value stocks. You can also buy shares tied to a growth stock index. Your purchases aren't limited to stock indexes. There are even shares tied to a bond index.

Like index funds, you won't get the highest return from exchange traded funds, but you will build a portfolio with considerable diversity. You won't get that diversity, however, from buying exchange traded funds tied to one particular index. For example, buying exchange traded funds containing a basket of large company stocks isn't enough. You also need to invest some of your wealth in the stocks of small companies, as well as other investments.

You can find data regarding the performance of exchange traded funds at www.morningstar.com. There are even exchange traded funds tied to the NASDAQ (www.nasdaq.com).

## PORTFOLIOS FOR THE SHELL-SHOCKED INVESTOR

Many financial advisers have offered very valuable suggestions for protecting your retirement. Larry Swedroe of St. Louis suggests this mixture of domestic stocks, which he calls the "coward's portfolio." He advises that you own at least four index funds focusing on:

- Large stocks in general
- Large value stocks
- Small stocks in general
- Small value stocks

To further diversify your coward's portfolio, Swedroe suggests adding an index fund that tracks real estate investment trusts.

Even if index funds aren't your cup of tea, you can still create a diversified portfolio. In the September 2002 issue of the *AARP Bulletin*, Peter Lynch of Fidelity Investments suggested a portfolio of mutual funds to diversify your assets. The portfolio included balanced funds, growth funds with stocks of large and small companies, value funds with stocks of large and small companies, technology funds, and overseas funds.

Other experts protect their clients' stock portfolio with a different approach. They suggest this breakdown:

- Large cap growth stock fund
- Large cap value stock fund
- Small and mid-cap growth stock fund
- Small and mid-cap value stock fund
- International stock fund

Even with the most diversified portfolio, however, there will be years when all of these categories will perform below expectations.

An all-weather fund is another interesting possibility for protecting your retirement. It is a single mutual fund that invests a fixed percentage in stocks, bonds, cash real estate, and precious metals. Some all-weather funds invest more aggressively in stocks and bonds, depending on the outlook for these investments. By investing more aggressively, this type of all-weather fund may offer a greater return, but it also is riskier.

## PROTECTION TIPS

The blueprint for protecting your investments doesn't have to be overly complex. Legendary investor John Bogle, who founded the Vanguard Group, said, "The secret of investing is there is no secret other than to put your money away regularly and intelligently and stay the course." As anyone who's watched their investments plummet during a bear market knows, staying the course isn't easy. It's especially difficult when you're putting money away regularly and losing ground in spite of your efforts. Nevertheless, you can sail through rough waters by charting your course, and eventually the wind will be at your back.

Systematic and ongoing investment programs are still the course to follow for most people. A simple and safe portfolio might be a nice mixture of stock index funds, bond index funds, and money market funds. Make sure you're buying stock mutual funds that use different styles of investing.

One of the best ways to protect your portfolio is to avoid being in a position where you must hold a fire sale of your stocks. When you have five to seven years of living expenses in cash, you can ride out almost any bear market. You aren't forced to sell stocks to pay your monthly bills. As you periodically rebalance your portfolio, make sure you keep enough cash on hand to keep you going through the next bear market.

# CHAPTER 19

# Lessons learned about
# protecting your retirement

DALE KOPPEL, A SPECIAL CORRESPONDENT FOR THE *SOUTH FLORIDA SUN-Sentinel*, wrote about Jack and Shirley Levin's retirement odyssey. After retiring in 1974, Jack, a physician, became restless and signed on to become the ship's doctor on a cruise line. He and his wife spent six months each year on board the ship. After nearly six years in that position with passengers calling him at all hours of the day and night, the Levins decided it would be much more enjoyable to cruise as a guest, not an employee.

Over twenty years later, the Levins are still cruising. Their most recent cruise was fifty-two days long. They still enjoy each other's company and reserve a table for two. Although the couple is more well-off than most, they do their best to save money. They never book an expensive cabin. The Levins found that Carnival Cruise Lines gives shipboard credits to shareholders, so they bought one hundred shares. Although cruising is expensive, the couple noted that it's cheaper than assisted living.

All of us know positive people who try to enjoy every minute of life and those who seem to have a chip on their shoulder. As you protect and rebuild your retirement, try to learn from the people who make the most of all the time they have left. Look for role models and mentors who are living the kind of retirement you want. Study them and ask how they managed to do it. Hopefully, you'll learn lessons from them, and you'll learn from the tough economic times we've been through in the past few years.

---

**TIPS FROM MARTIN NISSENBAUM, DIRECTOR, RETIREMENT PLANNING, ERNST & YOUNG**

Identify several retirement success models and why you believe they're successful. Interview them and discover their secrets.

Don't equate your retirement lifestyle with the standard of living you had in your last year of work.

---

## BACK TO BASICS

To protect your retirement, you may want to go back to basics. No matter what your age, your portfolio needs a nice mixture of stocks, bonds, and cash investments. Despite the roller-coaster ride of the last few years, stocks perform better than other investments over the long run. Bonds, even though they lose ground when interest rates rise, provide a safety net against a total meltdown of your portfolio during a bear market. Real estate investments will also be surprisingly resilient during a bear market.

Even though stocks and stock mutual funds will perform best over a ten- or twenty-year period, there will be times when your holdings are down significantly in value. Therefore, you need to have several years of living expenses in ready cash, so you won't need to sell your shares at their low point. And when the market is doing well, you can't keep riding the wave. Even in a bull market, look for opportunities to declare victory and move some of that money to more conservative investments.

Don't bet on a handful of stocks with the hope of hitting the jack-pot. You need a broad mix of stocks, not a half dozen that you bought based on a hot tip or an article you read in a magazine. You're also playing Russian roulette by investing heavily in your employer's stock.

Actively managed mutual funds put the decision of which stocks to buy and sell in the hands of the experts. The fund manager creates a portfolio aimed at achieving the investment objectives outlined in the prospectus. During a bear market, or even a bull market for that matter, the experts don't always do well in achieving those investment objectives.

Stop chasing the top-performing mutual fund. There's no assurance that the fund manager can repeat his or her performance, especially with much more money to invest from new investors. A more conservative approach is to buy index mutual funds. These funds have low expenses and don't rely on a manager to pick and choose which stocks to buy. Instead, the fund has a portfolio that is tied to a stock market index such as the S&P 500. If you were to buy an index fund tied to the S&P 500, you would own stock in 500 of the largest companies.

You can use the same approach when buying bonds. An index bond fund's portfolio is a mixture of bonds that make up a particular index. One possibility is a bond fund that tracks the entire bond market. Never-theless, even with all kinds of bonds in your portfolio, your total return (interest added to price increases or decreases) will fall as interest rates rise.

Exchange traded funds can give you some of the same diversity. Their expenses might be even lower than index funds. Whether you're buying exchange traded funds or index funds, make sure you're splitting your investment among different indexes that include both value stocks and growth stocks.

Don't overlook conservative mutual funds in your investment blue-print. For example, balanced funds are a little safer, because they are a mixture of stocks and bonds. Typically, balanced funds keep 60 percent of the investor's money in relatively conservative stocks.

Even if you hate to open the envelopes containing your 401(k) and IRA statements, tax-sheltered retirement accounts are still the best way to protect and rebuild your retirement. Put away as much as you can, and take advantage of the catch-up provisions that allow you to contribute more. Pay more attention from now on to your investment mix and rebalance periodically.

Dollar cost averaging is still the way to go, because some of the best financial experts can't predict the ideal time to buy and sell. Dollar cost averaging is an investment strategy that works particularly well when you're investing for the long haul in retirement savings plans. Instead of trying to pick the best time to invest, you put away the same amount at regular intervals into a mutual fund or some other investment vehicle.

The onus is now on you to save more for retirement. You can't count on your investment returns to make up for the fact that you love to spend money and hate to save it. To rebuild your retirement, you may need to stay at your job for longer than you originally thought.

To protect your retirement, stop looking for home runs and settle for singles and doubles. You won't get an 8 percent to 12 percent return on your investment, but you'll face the next bear market with more peace of mind and a steady rate of return. A 5 percent sure thing is better than a 15 percent maybe, especially if you lose sleep over it.

For that reason, a fixed annuity might be a better choice in some cases than a variable annuity. Although the return may not be spectacular, you're getting a predictable income each month. An annuity should help you sleep at night, not give you another investment to worry about because it's tied to the stock market.

If you're already retired and your investments aren't doing well, you need to spend less and save more. It might be time to reduce your overhead and cut back on your lifestyle. You may need to go back to work, hopefully part-time at a job you enjoy. Ideally, you'll find something that's challenging and rewarding.

Protecting your peace of mind is just as important as protecting your investments. Your health and your peace of mind are your most precious retirement assets. Worrying and being stressed out about money isn't going to help your physical and mental well-being.

## LESSONS LEARNED

Both novice and experienced investors learned difficult lessons from the first bear market of the twenty-first century. The obvious lesson we've learned is that the experts weren't kidding when they said to diversify. The real losers in the past few years were investors who put too much of their money in stock and invested too much in one or two companies that did poorly. Your commitment to diversity should begin today, even if it's just with new money that you're investing.

We've learned too that you may not be as diversified as you think. Your investments may be in a number of mutual funds, but they might own many of the same stocks. Many investors don't have any clue what holdings are in their mutual funds and if too many of them overlap.

To stay diversified, you need to take the asset allocation strategy seriously. This means rebalancing periodically and shifting assets from one class to another. Often this means shifting assets away from strong performers to underperforming assets. Although this goes against your intuition, it's the best way to reduce volatility in your portfolio.

We've learned that you can't buy stocks and hold them forever. You have to watch for signs that a company isn't what it used to be. A stock that's been around forever can be gone tomorrow.

Before the events of the early twenty-first century, there were financial planners who advised clients, even elderly ones, to remain heavily invested in stocks. As a result of their advice, you might find eighty-year-olds with too large a percentage of their assets in stocks. Eighty-year-olds may have a long life ahead of them, but only a small part of their portfolio should be in equities, preferably conservative stocks.

Although older people may still need a conservative stock portfolio to keep up with inflation, they often rely on their investments and not a paycheck to pay their bills. You should always have five to seven years in liquid investments, so you won't be forced to sell depressed stocks at the worst time.

Remember, however, that your time horizon isn't year one of your retirement. Hopefully, your retirement will last twenty years or longer, so some of your nest egg should be in stocks. A portion of your assets need to grow for year ten, year twenty, or even year forty of your retirement.

Financial planners may need to rethink some of the standard advice given in the past. You frequently heard them advise that it's silly to pay off a low-interest mortgage, since you'll make a far better rate of return in the stock market. People who opted for the market in lieu of paying off their mortgage lost a great deal of money, as well as the psychological lift that comes with unloading their home loan.

Financial expert Andrew Tobias has said that debt is for the first half of your life. Since most people retire during the second half of their life, be very careful about incurring debt as you approach retirement age. It's harder to pay off debt with a smaller income.

Another lesson learned is that retirement is not the time to overextend yourself. Although it's always dangerous to overextend yourself, there is less risk when you have a lifetime of earnings ahead of you. Retirement is not the time to take on big financial obligations, because you can't count on a larger income as you could have early in your career.

The bear market in the early twenty-first century showed investors that the market is no place for parking their money. Too many investors took their bonus, or profits from a house or rental property, and reinvested them with the hope of doubling their money quickly. They watched their windfall blow away.

Many of us learned that being rich on paper isn't nearly as good as having cash in the bank. You need to be quicker to lock in profits instead of anticipating a further increase in the value of your investment.

## DESIGNING YOUR OWN BLUEPRINT FOR RETIREMENT

Whether you're retired already, nearing retirement, or years away from retirement, you should be developing your own blueprint. Planning your retirement should be an activity you enjoy. Whether you're traveling on planes, trains, or automobiles, or sitting in your bathrobe, think about retirement and how rewarding it can be. If the traditional retirement age is too far off, plan for early retirement or financial independence, so each day will be your own.

You may need to reconstruct your perception of retirement and make adjustments. Decide what's truly important to you. Focus on your ideal retirement lifestyle. Map out what each day will be like. The first step is to dream it. The second step is to make the dream a reality.

Fill out an expense worksheet with how much you're spending. Don't depend on the old rule of thumb that you'll need 70 percent to 80 percent of your preretirement income to live on. It might be much more or much less, depending on the decisions you make.

Take control of your finances. You can't keep living like money is no object. Even Bill Gates doesn't buy everything he sees.

Much as you love your children, you shouldn't need to work forever, so they don't have to work at all. Too many people feel pressured to keep working because their children never became financially independent.

As much as you hate to look at your 401(k) and other financial statements, keep tabs on your portfolio. Make sure you distinguish between assets you can take without paying taxes, such as withdrawals from a Roth IRA, and assets that you can't get at without paying taxes.

Review your debts. Set up a home equity line of credit and hope you'll never need it. It's easier to get while you're still employed. Protect your credit rating because it can be extremely helpful in protecting your retirement.

Start the search for the perfect retirement area as early as possible in life. Whenever you travel on business or pleasure, think about whether this is a place you'd like to live in someday. If Florida is where you want to end up, visit every part of Florida, not just the tourist destinations. Don't revolve your decision around one particular couple you're friendly with or family members. Those people might not be around someday or may move.

Don't wish your life away, but imagine what it will be like to do whatever you wish on any given day. You can plan thoroughly for that time in life without sacrificing your current lifestyle and your dreams. You can protect and rebuild your retirement and live out your dreams.

401(k) retirement savings plan—A retirement plan that permits employees to make contributions on a pretax basis and defer taxes until withdrawn. Employers generally match all or a portion of the contribution.

403(b) retirement savings plan—A retirement plan that is similar to, but not exactly the same as, a 401(k) plan. It is offered to public school employees, as well as the employees of certain tax-exempt organizations. A 403(b) is sometimes called a Tax-Sheltered Annuity, or TSA.

457 plan—A deferred compensation plan for employees in the public sector.

aggressive growth funds—Mutual funds that invest in small or fast-growing companies. Their primary goal is capital gains, not dividends. Aggressive investments are likely to have wide swings in value.

all-weather fund—A single mutual fund that invests a fixed percentage in stocks, bonds, real estate, and cash investments. Some all-weather funds invest more aggressively in stocks and bonds, depending on the outlook for these investments, but the goal is to create a diverse portfolio.

annuitize—To convert the accumulated value of an annuity into a stream of income.

annuity—An investment contract between an investor and an insurance company. The annuity can be used to guarantee an income for a specified period of time.

asset allocation—The process of dividing your money among different types of assets such as stocks, bonds, and cash. This investment strategy is based on the assumption that various investments will do well at different times. Asset allocation is based upon your financial objectives and risk tolerance.

averaging down—Purchasing additional shares in a stock or mutual fund you already own when the shares drop in price from your earlier purchase.

balanced funds—Mutual funds that invest in a mix of bonds, preferred stock, and common stock. The goal is to blend stocks that will grow in value with income-producing securities. Investors in balanced funds have more protection against downturns in the stock market.

bear market—A stock market that is declining in value where investors are generally pessimistic.

blue-chip stocks—A common stock that is well-thought of, because it produces earnings in good times and bad.

boiler room—A temporary office filled with phones where salespeople call lists of prospects, hoping to talk them into buying worthless or greatly overpriced investments.

bond fund—A mutual fund that invests in bonds. Bond funds seek high current income by investing in debt securities including U.S. government securities.

bonds—Loans or debt issued by corporations or governmental entities to raise money. The issuer of a bond agrees to pay bondholders a specified amount of interest and to repay the principal at maturity.

brokerage firm—A firm that buys or sells securities for its own account or for its clients. It's also called a broker-dealer.

bull market—A stock market that is advancing rapidly where investors are generally optimistic.

callable CD—A Certificate of Deposit that allows the financial institution to end the agreement after a specified number of years. The financial institution will exploit this feature if interest rates go down significantly.

capital gain—The increase in value when the selling price is higher than the adjusted cost of an asset. The tax rate on capital gains has been decreased.

cash—Short-term investments that can be converted into cash quickly without losing principal, such as money market funds.

cash balance pension plans—A newer type of defined benefit plan that is portable and accrues benefits gradually. Conversions to cash balance pension plans may shortchange older workers.

certificate of deposit (CD)—An investment where the investor receives a fixed rate of interest for a specified period of time. CDs are issued by banks, savings and loans, credit unions, and brokerage firms. They are normally insured by the FDIC or the FSLIC, and there is usually a penalty for early withdrawal.

churning—Excessive trading in a client's account by a broker or salesperson.

COBRA—Consolidated Omnibus Budget Reconciliation Act. COBRA usually permits you to buy coverage from your former employer for eighteen months or more, depending upon your situation. Under COBRA, you pay the group rate, plus an administrative charge, and you don't get the employer's contribution common stock—Ownership in a company as reflected by shares. Common stockholders participate in the ownership of a company through dividends and appreciation in the value of their stock. They also share in the risk that the price of the stock will go down.

compound interest—Interest that is earned from both the principal and the interest on the principal. Compound interest may be calculated on a daily, monthly, quarterly, semiannual, or annual basis.

convertible corporate bonds—Corporate bonds that can be converted into stock.

corporate bonds—Bonds issued by corporations. They pay a higher interest rate than U.S. Treasury securities.

debt instrument—A classy name for a bond or an IOU.

defined benefit plan—A pension plan that specifies the amount the employee will receive after a specified number of years with the employer.

defined contribution plan—A form of a pension plan that specifies what the employee may contribute, rather than what the employee will receive after meeting the requirements of the plan. A 401(k) retirement savings plan is an example.

diversification—An investment strategy of putting money in different investment categories or different stocks to minimize risk.

dividend—A portion of a company's earnings paid out to stockholders.

dividend yield—The amount of money per share paid out to shareholders divided by the price of the stock.

dollar-cost averaging—An investment strategy where you invest a fixed dollar amount at regular intervals. You buy more shares when the price is low and fewer shares when prices are high. You're likely to end up with a favorable price per share.

Dow Jones Industrial Average—A price-weighted average of thirty actively traded blue-chip stocks. It is the oldest and most well-known stock market indicator.

durable power of attorney—A legal document that authorizes someone to be the agent or attorney-in-fact for another person. The authority continues, even if the principal becomes incapacitated or incompetent.

Employee Stock Ownership Plan (ESOP)—A retirement plan that permits the employee to invest in the stock of the employer.

equity investments—Investments that represent ownership such as stocks. They can be distinguished from assets that represent debt, such as bonds.

exchange traded funds—Shares that are bought and sold like stocks and represent ownership linked to a particular index. They resemble an index fund.

expense ratio—The ratio of a mutual fund's expenses to its assets.

Federal Deposit Insurance Corporation (FDIC)—An agency of the federal government that insures deposits up to $100,000 at commercial banks.

Federal Savings and Loan Insurance Corporation (FSLIC)—An agency of the federal government that insures deposits in savings and loans up to $100,000.

fund of funds—A mutual fund that invests in many other mutual funds. The fund of funds offers greater diversification than a traditional mutual fund. Expenses, however, are likely to be higher, because of the fees on the fund of funds and the expenses charged by the underlying funds.

GNMA—Also called Ginnie Mae. The Government National Mortgage Association issues bonds that are backed by a pool of mortgages.

government securities—Securities issued by a government to raise funds needed to pay expenses.

growth-and-income funds—A mutual fund that invests in income-producing securities such as bonds and dividend-paying stocks. The fund seeks capital appreciation and income.

growth funds—A mutual fund that seeks capital appreciation rather than current income. The investment objective is to buy stocks that will appreciate in value over the long term.

growth stocks—Companies whose earnings are expected to grow rapidly. The price of these stocks is relatively high compared to what the earnings are now.

guaranteed investment contract (GIC)—A contract that pays a fixed interest rate for a specified period of time, usually one to five years. A stable value fund, commonly offered as an investment option in retirement savings plans, usually invests in GICs from many different insurance companies.

high-yield bonds—These bonds are often called junk bonds. They pay a higher rate of interest, because they have a greater risk of default.

I bond—An inflation-indexed savings bond offered by the U.S. Treasury.

income funds—Mutual funds that invest primarily in bonds. They should not be confused with equity income funds, which invest primarily in dividend-paying stocks.

income stock—A stock that consistently pays a regular dividend to shareholders.

index mutual funds—A fund that uses the money pooled from all investors to match the performance of some broad market index. Index funds have low expense ratios and usually appeal to passive investors.

Individual Retirement Account (IRA)—A tax-sheltered account used to save for retirement. In addition to traditional IRAs, which offer an immediate tax deduction, Roth IRAs offer no tax deduction, but qualified withdrawals are tax-free.

international funds—Mutual funds that invest in companies that do business overseas. These funds are riskier than funds that invest in companies doing business in the United States.

junk bond—A bond that offers a higher yield, but with a more significant element of risk. Sometimes called a high-yield bond.

Keogh plan—A retirement plan for the self-employed. There are two types of Keoghs, a money purchase Keogh and a profit-sharing Keogh.

laddering—A strategy used when buying CDs and bonds, so that the investments reach maturity at regular intervals and the investor receives a steady stream of cash to spend or reinvest.

life cycle funds—Mutual funds that contain a premixed portfolio of stocks, bonds, and cash. The mixture is based on your age, risk temperament, and/or estimated retirement date.

lifestyle funds—Also known as life cycle or life stage funds. A premixed portfolio of stocks, bonds, and cash. The mixture is based on your age, risk temperament and/or estimated retirement date.

liquidity—Investments that can be converted into cash quickly without losing your principal. Because retirees often depend upon their investments for income rather than a paycheck, they need a certain amount of liquidity to ensure that their needs are met for the immediate future.

living trust—A legal document that helps you control your assets while you're alive, as well as after you die. It is used as a means to avoid probate, which can delay the disposition of your property.

living will—A document that states in general terms what kind of medical care you want and don't want.

load—A commission or sales charge that may be applied to investments such as mutual funds. It may take the form of an upfront load or a back-end load. Some funds apply a 12b-1 fee, which is a charge for marketing expenses and distribution.

lump sum distribution—Payment to an employee of the entire amount in her pension or retirement account, rather than in a series of payments.

maturity—The date on which a bond or CD comes due.

money market fund—A mutual fund that invests in short-term debt. Although these funds are extremely safe, they are not insured by the FDIC. They are run by mutual fund companies and aren't the same as the money market account offered by your bank or savings and loan.

Monte Carlo methodology—A mathematical approach that examines potential market scenarios and is used to determine whether a particular withdrawal rate is likely to exhaust your nest egg.

municipal bond—A debt obligation of a state, city, school district, or public entity. The interest paid is usually not subject to federal income taxes. The income from these bonds may, however, be included in determining whether you'll pay tax on your Social Security benefit.

mutual fund—An investment that pools together money from many investors. Mutual funds are professionally managed and invested according to the guidelines outlined in the prospectus.

phased retirement—A program, either formal or informal, that allows employees to work fewer hours during the period leading up to full retirement. Many universities now offer phased retirement to professors. Phased retirement might take the form of part-time employment, job sharing, or a formally structured program.

Ponzi scheme—One of the oldest investment scams. The victims' money is never invested. The first investors are paid out of funds swindled from subsequent investors.

portfolio—A group of securities held by an individual or institution.

preferred stock—A type of ownership in a corporation that guarantees fixed dividends, but no right to vote. In the event a company is liquidated, preferred stockholders are given preference over owners of common stock.

principal—The amount of money that is invested or borrowed.

prospectus—A document that provides a thorough description of a mutual fund such as the objective, how it invests money, and the fees charged.

rate of return—The return on an investment, usually expressed as a percentage.

rebalancing—Shifting assets from one class to another to assure diversification of your portfolio. For the asset allocation strategy to work, you need to rebalance your portfolio periodically.

risk tolerance—Your ability to deal with the risks associated with any investment. High tolerance for risk means you're able to deal psychologically with an investment that may be highly volatile. Low tolerance for risk means that you're not well-suited to deal with an investment that fluctuates significantly in value.

savings bond—An IOU issued by the U.S. Treasury. Unlike other Treasury securities, savings bonds cannot be sold or traded in a secondary market.

Savings Incentive Match Plan for Employees (SIMPLE IRA)—A defined contribution plan for the self-employed and companies with one hundred employees or fewer.

sector fund—A mutual fund that invests in companies in specific industries such as healthcare or technology.

Securities and Exchange Commission (SEC)—The federal agency that regulates the securities market and oversees the securities laws.

security—An investment such as stocks or bonds.

Simplified Employee Pension (SEP IRA)—A defined contribution plan designed for the self-employed or a small business.

Spider—A very popular exchange traded fund, which stands for Standard & Poor's Depository Receipt or Spider (SPDR). Spiders track the value of an S&P index such as the S&P 500, which is comprised of large company stocks. There are also Spiders that track the S&P MidCap 400 stocks. Spiders are bought and sold like stocks with all of the same risks. The symbol is SPY.

stable value fund—An investment option offered in many retirement savings plans. The stable value fund invests in Guaranteed Investment Contracts (GICs) from many insurance companies.

stock—Ownership in a company reflected by the number of shares. The person who owns the stock is a stockholder or shareholder.

stock fund—A mutual fund that invests exclusively in equities.

tax-deferred investment—An investment where taxes are postponed until withdrawal of the funds or when the investment matures. A tax-deferred investment is different from a tax-free investment.

time horizon—The amount of time you have until you need the money invested. Generally, the shorter your time horizon, the less risk you should be taking with the money.

TIPS (Treasury Inflation-Protected Securities)—Securities issued by the U.S. Treasury. Although the interest rate stays the same, the principal is adjusted semiannually based on changes in the Consumer Price Index. They are also known as Treasury Inflation-Indexed Securities.

total return—The percentage showing how much you made or lost on an investment during a specified time frame. The total return assumes that all interest, dividends, and capital gains are reinvested. It's a combination of yield and the change in share price.

total stock market fund—An index fund that tracks the Wilshire 5000 index of most regularly traded U.S. stocks.

tracking stocks—Stocks that are tied to a single business within a company. You don't get the same ownership rights as regular stocks. Tracking stocks allow you to invest in a potentially high-growth segment of the company without worrying about the other businesses.

Treasury bills—Short-term government securities with maturity dates of no more than one year. Also called T-bills.

Treasury securities—Bills, notes, and bonds that are the direct obligations of the U.S. government.

value stocks—Stocks that appear to be a bargain, because they are unpopular with investors, but have the potential to turn around. They are perceived to be selling for less than their true value, based on the company's earnings and book value.

variable annuity—A contract purchased from an insurance company, generally used to accumulate money for retirement. Earnings accumulate on a tax-deferred basis. The purchaser of an annuity chooses how the money is invested.

viatical settlements—Lump sum payments to individuals who are terminally ill in exchange for the death benefit of their life insurance policy.

will—A legal document that transfers assets at death.

yield—The dividend or interest rate on an investment. It's often used incorrectly to mean total return.

zero coupon bond—A bond issued at a discount that increases in value until reaching maturity. Although interest is not paid out to the bond holder, you pay taxes on the income as if it were being paid out.